T

SHAKE

CONSPIRACY

A most lamentable epic
romantic tragic comedy

by Andrew Shepherd

SAMUEL FRENCH

ISBN 978-0-573-13285-8

concordtheatricals.co.uk
concordtheatricals.com

FOR PRODUCTION ENQUIRIES

UNITED KINGDOM AND WORLD
EXCLUDING NORTH AMERICA
licensing@concordtheatricals.co.uk
020-7054-7298

NORTH AMERICA
info@concordtheatricals.com
1-866-979-0447

Each title is subject to availability from Concord Theatricals, depending upon country of performance.

This work is published by Samuel French, an imprint of Concord Theatricals. Ltd

USE OF COPYRIGHTED MUSIC

USE OF COPYRIGHTED THIRD-PARTY MATERIALS

IMPORTANT BILLING AND CREDIT REQUIREMENTS

THE SHAKESPEARE CONSPIRACY was first performed over the course of two productions at Chelsea Theatre, London in June 2011 and November 2012. The Directors were Chris Hislop, Jack Bowman, Designer Zahra Mansouri, Lighting Designer Sherry Coenen, Sound Designers Gustav Mahler, Tshari King, Assistant Directors Kuba Drewa, Sarah Meadows, Fight Sequences Matt Gardner, Assistant Designers Jaemi Bermudez, Abi Bath, Alex Kerr, Produced by ACSRandom. The cast was as follows:

MARTIN	Andrew London	Andrew London
VALENTINE	Tom Ashley	Will Bryant
JULES	Alethea Steven	Alethea Steven
TYBALT	Jay Carrington	Danny Solomon
GARFIELD OBERON	James Ellis	Richard Armah
PUCK	Joanne Gale	Nayomie Karen
IAGO	Andrew Shepherd	Andrew Shepherd
EDMUND	Lee White	Lee White
LADY MACBETH	Alexa Brown	Leonora Barton
RICHARD III	Matt Gardner	Alexander Pankhurst
BENEDICK	Jack Baldwin	Jack Baldwin
BEATRICE	Libby Evans	Libby Evans
THREE SISTERS	Lynne Rodgers	Francesca Cicic
	Melanie Loudonsack	Charlotte Mack
	Leanne Wigginton	Holly McClay
HELENA	Holly Janowski	Holly Janowski

CHARACTERS

(in order of appearance)

MARTIN SHAKESPEARE – A travel agent

VALENTINE – Martin's best friend

JULES – An agent for the RSC

TYBALT – A hitman

GARFIELD OBERON – Artistic Director of the RSC

PUCK – An agent for the RSC

(ALOYSIUS ARCHIBALD) IAGO – An evil genius

EDMUND BASTARD SON OF GLOUCESTER – A bastard

LADY (ANTONIA) MACBETH – Iago's sister

RICHARD III – Lady Macbeth's son

BENEDICK – An agent for the RSC

BEATRICE – An agent for the RSC

HELENA – From A Midsummer Night's Dream

THREE SISTERS – From Macbeth (Also playing Partygoers/Agents/Prison Guards/Trainees)

VILLAINS & HEROES – Played by members of the cast

Please cast as inclusively, imaginatively and openly as you want. Roles can be doubled/tripled dependent on your budget.

SETTING

The "Real world" is set in modern times.
The "Theatre world" is timeless.

AUTHOR'S NOTES

It began in the bath, as many good things do. A thought popping into reality – what would happen if Richard III gatecrashed into *A Midsummer Night's Dream* and started wooing Helena instead of Lady Anne, taking the place of the spurning Demetrius? Once the first boundary had been crossed, the possibilities were endless – especially if you combine them with a love of superhero movies.

Now, a key theme in those movies is that the stakes are always HUGE, the same can be said for Shakespeare and the best comedies. This is not a play to be underplayed, understated or taken at all seriously... as long as you play it completely seriously and believe that the world is about to end. You need to lean into the theatricality, silliness and the epic.

But you don't necessarily have to do it on a massive budget. We certainly didn't in the first instance, but we used all the theatrical tools in our imagination and arsenal to create a sense of scale.

I've often believed if Shakespeare were alive today, they'd be writing the big movie/TV hits – re-read *Henry IV parts I, II* and *Henry V* and tell me it's not a superhero trilogy. Then there's the definitive doomed teen romance (*Romeo & Juliet*), the original romantic comedy (*Much Ado About Nothing*) and the greatest supervillain of them all... Iago. A man who, but with a few well chosen words, a brilliant and dangerous mind, and an understanding of the frailties of human nature brought down the best of us – some people just want to watch the world burn...

I'm sharing this because it's all in here. There's something for everyone – from the purists to the Easter Egg hunters to those of you who've never met William Shakespeare. It's also a classic hero's quest, where an ordinary person becomes truly extraordinary when they realise their potential. It's about the power of love and imagination. And for the more academic out there it could be argued that the whole thing smacks of a metatheatrical experiment which tries to play around with archetypal tropes, but cannot as every character must behave as it was originally written, all wrapped up in a five act structure that seems familiar to those of a Bardic disposition... but only if you're in to that kind of thing.

How should it be performed? However you want but *only* if is done with joy, imagination, collaboration, silliness, kindness, compassion and with the only people in mind who really matter... your audience.

Have fun, I did writing it...

ACS

For my Father, who gave me the gift of Shakespeare

PART ONE

ACT ONE

(I.i)

(Darkness. The stage is divided into two areas: the "real world" and the "theatre world".)

*(***MUSIC: GUSTAV MAHLER'S ["MOVEMENT V. IM TEMPO DES SHERZO"]*** *. Giving the feeling of an epic movie opening. Lights up on a young man,* **MARTIN** *(in the theatre world) who sits with his head buried in his hands.)*

(A faint light comes up on the real world revealing two characters observing **MARTIN.** *One is standing wearing a long coat and is holding a trilby, the other is wearing a ridiculous woolly hat with a suit. The man in the coat puts on his hat and they both exit, as the lights fade on them.)*

(The lights change and come up fully on the theatre world. **MARTIN***'s friend* **VALENTINE** *swaggers on drinking from a bottle of champagne singing.)*

---

* A licence to produce THE SHAKESPEARE CONSPIRACY and use GUSTAV MAHLER'S [MOVEMENT V. IM TEMPO DES SHERZO] does not include a performance licence for any third-party or copyrighted recordings. Licensees should create their own.

VALENTINE.

HAPPY BIRTHDAY TO YOU! HAPPY BIRTHDAY TO YOU!
HAPPY BIRTHDAY DEAR MARTIN WHO KEEPS ON FALLING IN LOVE WITH THE WRONG WOMEN DESPITE HIS FRIENDS INSISTING THEY DON'T REALLY LOVE HIM AND JUST WANT TO BE FRIENDS AND NOT GETTING BACK TO YOU ISN'T BECAUSE THEY'RE BUSY IT'S BECAUSE THEY'RE PROBABLY NOT INTO YOU...
HAPPY BIRTHDAY TO YOU!

(**VALENTINE** *offers* **MARTIN** *the champagne.* **MARTIN** *speaks with his head still in his hands.)*

MARTIN. I'm not going

VALENTINE. It's your party.

MARTIN. I don't care, Valentine, I'm not going

VALENTINE. You can't sulk here all night

MARTIN. Watch me

VALENTINE. She's not worth it

MARTIN. She was the one

VALENTINE. Just like all the others

MARTIN. Rosie's different

VALENTINE. She likes girls?

MARTIN. She's... virtuous

VALENTINE. You take three months to get to second base and the day after she tells you she's thinking of joining a convent

MARTIN. Our relationship was deeper than that

VALENTINE. You'd choose a life of chastity to be near a god-fearing feminist with the sexual charisma of a dead squirrel because you thought you love her.

MARTIN. I *did* love her, Valentine.

VALENTINE. You have no concept of love

MARTIN. Coming from the man whose idea of romance is to ask if they've got any friends who want to join in.

VALENTINE. And I rise with a huge… smile every morning.

MARTIN. There's no feeling in your life

VALENTINE. Oh there's plenty of feeling… with me it's Valentine's Day every day…

MARTIN. You don't understand

VALENTINE. Just come to your party, get outlandishly pissed, dance like it's the end of the world and we'll find you someone to ride you all the way into next week.

MARTIN. I'm not that kind of person

VALENTINE. Then at least act like it for a night. Love has screwed you over too many times, my friend. Brace yourself, take it like a man, flip it over and give it the treatment it fully deserves.

MARTIN. I won't enjoy myself

VALENTINE. Then I'll have fun for the both of us.

MARTIN. I'm not dancing

(**VALENTINE** *helps* **MARTIN** *up.)*

VALENTINE. Nay, gentle Romeo, we must have you dance

MARTIN. What did you say?

(A momentary pause.)

VALENTINE. Nothing – just hot air

(**VALENTINE** *puts his arm around* **MARTIN** *and leads him off.)*

MARTIN. I had the strangest dream last night

VALENTINE. So did I – which reminds me – you should call your mother.

(I.ii)

(They exit. Party music plays. The lights shift as a young lady,* **JULES**, *enters wearing a tattered pair of angel wings. She is holding a half-drunk bottle of champagne and a bunch of roses. Her mascara has run down her face. She takes a large swig of champagne, and begins to tear apart the roses muttering various curses and snide remarks under her breath,* **MARTIN** *re-enters with a small glass of champagne. He is holding a number of letters, which he proceeds to tear apart muttering various curses and snide remarks. They become aware of each other's presence and turn towards each other and look away suddenly.)*

MARTIN. Did my heart love 'til now?

JULES. What did you say?

MARTIN. Nothing

JULES. I thought you said, "Did my heart love 'til now"

MARTIN. Why would I say that?

JULES. Must be hearing things

MARTIN. Must be

JULES. Sorry

MARTIN. No problemo

---

* A licence to produce THE SHAKESPEARE CONSPIRACY does not include a performance licence for any third-party or copyrighted music. Licensees should create an original composition or use music in the public domain. For further information, please see Music Use Note on page iii.

(**MARTIN** *winces at his own cliché. They go back to their respective property destruction.* **JULES** *looks up.)*

JULES. That which we call a rose by any other name, would smell as sweet

MARTIN. Were you talking to me?

JULES. No

MARTIN. Sorry

JULES. No problem... o

(**JULES** *walks up to* **MARTIN**.*)*

Do you believe in love at first sight?

MARTIN. No

(She grabs and kisses him. They pull apart.)

JULES. Sorry

MARTIN. That's OK

JULES. My life's a bit crazy at the moment

MARTIN. Tell me about it

JULES. Two households... both alike in... no... do you like poetry?

MARTIN. No

(**JULES** *grabs and kisses him again. She pulls apart.)*

JULES. My last guy loved poetry. That's all he was interested in, that and – he was dull.

MARTIN. Why did you go out with him?

JULES. The sex was mind blowing

MARTIN. How... lovely

(**JULES** *laughs.*)

JULES. Is that the best you can come back with?

MARTIN. This usually doesn't happen to me

JULES. Where are you from?

MARTIN. Stratford

JULES. What brought you to London?

MARTIN. I left my wife

JULES. You're married?

MARTIN. No – I'm sorry – I completely made that up

(**JULES** *looks blank.*)

I was trying to be more... I came to London to seek my fortune

(**JULES** *smiles brightly.*)

JULES. What do you do?

MARTIN. I'm a travel agent

JULES. You're so normal!

(**JULES** *grabs and kisses him again.*)

MARTIN. I was going to say boring – but if it does it for you –

JULES. I love it! Makes a nice change from...

(*A pause.*)

MARTIN. I'm Martin

(**JULES** *looks startled.*)

JULES. Jules

MARTIN. Any chance I could get your number?

JULES. No. I'm sorry – this was a mistake – you should go –

MARTIN. But...

*(**JULES** turns away. **MARTIN** thinks about to say something but is interrupted by **VALENTINE** stumbling out.)*

VALENTINE. There you are! I say – has young Martin found himself a birthday *(**JULES** glances at **VALENTINE** who stops in his track; **JULES** turns away again.)* – present

MARTIN. Do you know each other?

*(**VALENTINE** goes up to **MARTIN** and ushers him off towards the party.)*

VALENTINE. Oh no mate – it's just I can smell the crazy ones from a mile off and I've found some Italian twins inside – I'll be along in a sec...

*(**VALENTINE** shoves **MARTIN** offstage and turns on **JULES**, instantly sober and furious.)*

What are you doing here?! Do you any idea how dangerous the situation is?

JULES. Is it him?

VALENTINE. We'll discuss it later

JULES. I'm so sorry –

*(Any further conversation is interrupted by screaming and general panic backstage. Three terrified (female) partygoers spill out onto the stage followed by **MARTIN**, with a sword at his neck held by a man in dark Elizabethan costume (he is a hitman called **TYBALT** but we do not know this yet). **JULES** slips away unseen.)*

MARTIN. Mate! I think you ordered the wrong stripper

(Silence. **VALENTINE** *steps forward and quietly draws a concealed rapier behind* **MARTIN**'*s back.* **TYBALT** *releases* **MARTIN**. **MARTIN** *grabs his neck.)*

He cut me! He actually drew blood! He –

*(***MARTIN** *notices* **VALENTINE**'*s sword.)*

What? What's going on?

*(***VALENTINE** *ignores* **MARTIN** *and begins to circle* **TYBALT**.*)*

Why are you holding a sword?

VALENTINE. Because he is

MARTIN. Yeah but... who carries around swords these days?

VALENTINE. Run

MARTIN. Why?

VALENTINE. Please Martin – no more questions – just run

MARTIN. Not until you put your sword down...

VALENTINE. If I do that, he's going to kill you

MARTIN. Me? Why would he...

*(***TYBALT** *makes a sudden lunge for* **MARTIN**. **VALENTINE** *intercepts it and there is a brief and violent sword fight. As quickly as it happens the two fighters break apart.)*

What the hell is going on?!

*(***VALENTINE** *&* **TYBALT** *fight again,* **TYBALT** *is disarmed,* **VALENTINE** *goes to kill him. Without thinking* **MARTIN** *run towards them.)*

Gentlemen for shame – forbear this outrage!

*(***VALENTINE** *turns in astonishment towards* **MARTIN**, *while at the same time* **TYBALT** *pulls out a dagger and stabs* **VALENTINE**. *There is some screaming followed by a stunned silence.* **VALENTINE** *looks down at his wound, and back up at* **MARTIN**. *He smiles.)*

VALENTINE. Tis nothing... a scratch

(He collapses, **MARTIN** *catches him.)*

MARTIN. Valentine!

VALENTINE. *(Struggling to speak.)* It has begun... I'm so sorry Martin...

MARTIN. Somebody call an ambulance! You've got nothing to be sorry about – you're going to be OK –

VALENTINE. ... 'tis not so deep as a well, nor so wide as a church door; but 'tis enough 'twill serve...

MARTIN. You're going into shock, Valentine – just stay with me

VALENTINE. I am peppered I warrant, for this world... my name... isn't Valentine

MARTIN. What?

*(***GARFIELD OBERON** *&* **PUCK** *enter – they are the same people we saw at the beginning.* **VALENTINE** *looks past* **MARTIN** *and directly at them.)*

VALENTINE. A plague on both your houses

*(**VALENTINE** dies. **MARTIN** lays down his body. He slowly stands in utter disbelief, turns and –)*

GARFIELD. There will be time to mourn his passing Martin. For now you must come with us.

(I.iii)

*(***GARFIELD*** turns and walks into the real world.* **PUCK** *goes up, takes a stunned* **MARTIN** *by the arm and leads them both in* **GARFIELD***'s wake.* **GARFIELD** *nods at the Partygoers, who instantly snap out of their shocked state to become Agents for the RSC, turning the real world into an office space and then moving over to the theatre world to dispose of* **VALENTINE***'s body. They also return to add background to the RSC office.* **PUCK** *leads* **MARTIN** *to a seat.* **GARFIELD** *meanwhile has removed his hat, which makes it a lot clearer he is also wearing an eye patch, taken out a decanter of brandy and two glasses out, poured out two healthy measures and places one in* **MARTIN***'s hand.)*

GARFIELD. Drink that, it'll help with the shock

*(***MARTIN*** drinks automatically,* **GARFIELD** *picks up the other glass.)*

One of my finest agents. We shall all miss him

MARTIN. Agents? Who are you?

GARFIELD. My name is Garfield Oberon; I am the Artistic Director of the Royal Shakespeare Company.

*(***GARFIELD*** downs the brandy. Pause.)*

MARTIN. Is this a sick joke?

GARFIELD. I really wish it was

MARTIN. What has the RSC got to do with Valentine being murdered?

GARFIELD. Everything. To begin with your friend –

MARTIN. Valentine... his name is... was... Valentine

GARFIELD. His name was Mercutio.

MARTIN. Mercutio… the RSC's a theatre company.

GARFIELD. The RSC is a branch of the government. It is dedicated to the protection of Shakespeare's work and characters from threats within and without of this world.

PUCK. We're a bit like MI6 but with better costumes

*(**MARTIN** is at a loss for words.)*

GARFIELD. The key question, Martin, is what is the difference between reality and fiction? Reality is the physical and emotional perception of the world we wake up to and interact in. Fiction is the realms of imagination expressed in various means, to entertain those within the immediate vicinity. But what if reality is, in fact, fiction? Furthermore what someone might believe to be fiction could actually be reality. And once you know the answer to that question we can address the matter in hand: William Shakespeare.

*(**MARTIN** stares blankly at **GARFIELD** for a moment.)*

MARTIN. What?

GARFIELD. Shakespeare's characters are real.

(Pause.)

MARTIN. Why didn't you say that in the first place?

PUCK. He likes the sound of his own voice

GARFIELD. Do you mind?

PUCK. Sorry

MARTIN. Shakespeare's characters are real?

GARFIELD. Yes

MARTIN. Living, breathing, flesh & blood, walking around like you and me real?

GARFIELD. Yes

MARTIN. I can't believe I'm asking this – how did that happen?

PUCK. We have no idea!

GARFIELD. No one can quite explain it on, say, a cross – dimensional, metaphysical, actual scientific-based rationale; but it is... as it is.

(Slight pause.)

MARTIN. What?

PUCK. Four hundred years ago William Shakespeare brought his characters to life.

MARTIN. *(Sarcastically.)* A bloke walks around Elizabethan London telling everyone he's Hamlet, Prince of Denmark...

GARFIELD. That's classified – how do you know that?

PUCK. Elizabeth's spymaster, Francis Walsingham, put together a group of his finest agents under the leadership of Richard Burbage. On the surface a simple acting troupe called the Queen's Players, underneath the first guardians of Shakespeare's work and characters.

MARTIN. A prototype RSC –

GARFIELD. Excellent, Martin, you're catching on fast

MARTIN. Thanks

PUCK. I don't think he believes us

MARTIN. No, but don't let that stop you.

GARFIELD. It is the truth

MARTIN. Why does the rest of the world think the RSC is just a theatre company?

PUCK. No one would believe us

MARTIN. And I'm expected me to believe you because...?

GARFIELD. Because why would be choose the worst moment in your life so far to tell you a "sick joke" and because your best friend chose, in his dying moments, to tell you his name wasn't Valentine.

(Silence.)

PUCK. That was cheery

GARFIELD. Shut up, Robin

MARTIN. Robin... as in?

GARFIELD. Meet Robin Goodfellow, from *A Midsummer Night's Dream.*

*(***PUCK** *takes her hat off to reveals a pair of horns protruding from the top of his head, and removes her coat to reveal his costume. She lowers his head towards* **MARTIN.***)*

PUCK. You can touch them if you like –

GARFIELD. Robin is also known as Puck or Hobgoblin

PUCK. Good Luck!

GARFIELD. Or Sweet Puck

PUCK. Good Luck! How many times have I told you to stop doing that?!

GARFIELD. Apologies

MARTIN. Why do you say "good luck"?

PUCK. Those that Hobgoblin call me, or Sweet Puck... I sweep their houses and wish them all good luck.

MARTIN. Hobgoblin?

PUCK. Good Luck!

MARTIN. Sweet Puck

PUCK. Good Luck!

MARTIN. Hob –

PUCK. Stop it!

MARTIN. *(Sarcastically.)* Aren't you going to sweep my house?

PUCK. I have – twice – his too – your wife is in one of her moods again, sir.

GARFIELD. What is it this time?

PUCK. She says "if you have to ask..."

MARTIN. You didn't leave the room

PUCK. I'm very fast

MARTIN. Really...

PUCK. On your browser history there's a subscription to big –

MARTIN. Oh my God – Shakespeare's characters are real! How fast can you –?

PUCK. I can put a girdle round the earth in forty minutes.

MARTIN. You're actually Puck.

PUCK. Yes, yes, thou speakst aright, I am that merry wanderer of the –

GARFIELD. He's got the point

MARTIN. And you're the "real" Oberon?

GARFIELD. No – it's just my name

MARTIN. Valentine – Mercutio – Mercutio was?

GARFIELD. From *Romeo and Juliet*

MARTIN. If he's dead – the play – the whole plot will be altered

GARFIELD. To destroy Mercutio completely you'd have to burn or rewrite the original manuscript.

MARTIN. He's still alive?

GARFIELD. Once killed in the real world, characters revert to the state they were written as. I'm sorry – the Mercutio you knew is dead.

MARTIN. Couldn't he be rewritten to remember me?

GARFIELD. Anything is possible in theatre. That's why all the original drafts are locked away in a location only accessible to the incumbent Artistic Director.

MARTIN. Why only him?

PUCK. Or her

(**GARFIELD** *gives* **PUCK** *a look.)*

GARFIELD. To prevent a repeat of "*The Macbeth Incident*". The work of the coldest, most devious manipulator to walks the face of the globe. The greatest villain ever created

MARTIN. Macbeth?

PUCK. Iago

MARTIN. But he's in *Othello*.

GARFIELD. So was his sister

MARTIN. Iago never had a sister

GARFIELD. She disappeared in 1605 and reappeared a year later in an early draft called *The History of That Most Excellente and Good King Macbeth of Scotland* claiming to be Macbeth's wife, turning a historical romp into a supernatural pot-boiler.

MARTIN. Lady Macbeth is Iago's sister –

PUCK. Aloysius Archibald and Antonia

GARFIELD. Iago formed a syndicate of villains from the Bard's work. They were responsible for the rise in crime around the Southwark area during the time. It was only when Iago started meddling with the other plays that Shakespeare himself put two and two together and felt compelled to act.

PUCK. Shakespeare's villains were rounded up and placed in a custom-made maximum-security prison.

GARFIELD. You call it the Globe.

MARTIN. The Globe's a... oh never mind... why is Iago so dangerous?

GARFIELD. Iago is planning to break the rules of theatre which we theorise will cause a chain reaction that will destroy humanity. The rules of theatre are a force more powerful than you could possibly imagine.

MARTIN. How's he's going to pull that off?

PUCK. We have no idea

GARFIELD. We know it's got something to do with you

MARTIN. Me? Why?

GARFIELD. Your name

MARTIN. Martin?

GARFIELD. Your last name

(A slight pause.)

MARTIN. Don't be ridiculous

GARFIELD. Martin Shakespeare... you are the last living descendant of William Shakespeare. In your veins flows the blood protecting the world from certain destruction.

MARTIN. Hang on – his son died...

GARFIELD. We faked Hamnet's death, after we heard the Last Descendant Prophecy.

MARTIN. Oh great there's a prophecy...

PUCK. Two households, both alike in dignity

Within this wooden O, this throne of kings

If blood should fall from last descendant on't

They shall be freed to cross the mortal realm.

With inky blots and rotten parchment bonds:

Shall he that plays the villain end this world.

When all seems lost the heroes he'll bring back

Then do the state some service, smite him thus

To be or not to be it must be braved

With end it starts again, ere world is saved

(Silence. **MARTIN** *stands up.)*

GARFIELD. Where are you going?

MARTIN. Home

GARFIELD. Why?

MARTIN. To forget this ever happened

GARFIELD. You can't, you're our only hope

MARTIN. I'm not the saviour of mankind. I'm a travel agent from Stratford. Can I go now?

(An agent places a large sheaf of papers on the table.)

PUCK. OK – could you sign these before you go?

MARTIN. What are they?

PUCK. Standard disclaimers clearing the RSC of any responsibility for your certain death. If you could sign here, here, here and here, initial here and here – oh and here – you can be on your way

MARTIN. You're trying to intimidate me

GARFIELD. If you leave without our protection, you'll be dead in two hours

MARTIN. Who's planning to kill me?

PUCK. Iago. The execution will be carried out by a hitman called Tybalt. Tybalt killed Mercutio.

(**MARTIN** *hesitates.)*

GARFIELD. At least see why Iago wants to kill you

(**MARTIN** *considers his options and sits.* **GARFIELD** *puts on his hat and starts to walk over to the theatre world.)*

MARTIN. Where are you going?

GARFIELD. Into the theatre world

(I.iv)

(Lights up on the theatre world. Classical music plays quietly – the kind of music meeting a supervillain in prison. The other two agents have now turned into prison warders, and have turned the theatre world into a prison.* **IAGO** *is standing in the shadows with his back to the audience, in prison garb. He is conducting an imaginary orchestra.)*

MARTIN. Is that –?

PUCK. The most dangerous criminal mastermind in the history of the world: Aloysius Archibald Iago.

MARTIN. Can he hear us?

PUCK. No, this is Garfield's memory.

*(**GARFIELD** enters the theatre world. Without turning around **IAGO** raises a hand, which silences the music and speaks.)*

IAGO. Good evening Garfield.

GARFIELD. Good evening Aloysius

IAGO. Only my mother addressed me by that name, and she died shortly afterwards.

GARFIELD. You're fictional, Iago, you never had a mother.

*(**IAGO** slowly turns towards **GARFIELD**.)*

---

*A licence to produce THE SHAKESPEARE CONSPIRACY does not include a performance licence for any third-party or copyrighted music. Licensees should create an original composition or use music in the public domain. For further information, please see Music Use Note on page iii.

IAGO. True... but if I had one she would have met an unfortunate end in my early teens.

GARFIELD. You've been watching Netflix again

IAGO. So much high quality drama, so little time. Have a seat.

(They both sit.)

Congratulations on the promotion by the way.

GARFIELD. Thank you

IAGO. I hoped they'd make you Artistic Director. At last, I said to myself, a true artist.

GARFIELD. You're too kind – now I must –

IAGO. No, no, no, this may be your first visit as Director, but if you consult your Shakespeare Protocol Guide, page four – paragraph twelve: "When addressing a particularly scheming and clever villain it is necessary to exchange meaningless pleasantries to break the ice"

GARFIELD. Very well *(Pause.)* How are you?

IAGO. Never been better. How are you?

GARFIELD. Fine.

IAGO. What's your poison?

GARFIELD. What?

IAGO. Gin? Whisky? Châteauneuf-du-Pape?

GARFIELD. I'm on duty

IAGO. Nonsense, I've been experimenting with cocktails – you simply must try my latest

(He clicks his fingers, one of the warders comes forward with a tray and two cocktail glasses containing bright green fluid. **IAGO** *takes the glasses.)*

Thank you, sister

(He hands one to **GARFIELD**.*)*

Now you have to be completely honest with me

*(***GARFIELD** *takes a sip, and splutters.)*

GARFIELD. What's in it?

IAGO. Vodka martini with a splash of crème de menthe – I call it the Green Eyed Monster *(Takes a sip.)* ...how's your wife?

GARFIELD. She's... fine

IAGO. Ha... I like not that...

GARFIELD. She's fine... perfectly happy, everything's fine. My private life is none of your business

IAGO. Naturally. But things sometimes do filter through.

GARFIELD. What things?

IAGO. None of my business

GARFIELD. Have you heard something?

IAGO. Nothing, nothing, except... malicious gossip – that's all.

GARFIELD. Exactly

IAGO. Probably jealous you got the job... happily married –

GARFIELD. Very happily –

IAGO. I'm so happy for you both, although –

GARFIELD. What? What?

IAGO. They do say there's no smoke without fire

GARFIELD. Who says?

IAGO. I hate to be the one to tell you, but better you find out before it gets out of hand, I suppose...

GARFIELD. What have they been saying?

(**IAGO** *leans towards* **GARFIELD.**)

IAGO. Look to Nick Ramsbotham.

(There is a slight pause and **GARFIELD** *starts to laugh.)*

GARFIELD. Nick? Old Nick Rambotham! You had me going for a second. Nick Ramsbotham is our next door neighbour. He breeds donkeys and lives with a man called Peter. So you see... you've got it all wrong.

IAGO. Have you met this... Peter?

GARFIELD. Er. No

IAGO. How can you be sure "Peta's" not a woman?

GARFIELD. I don't know, I've never asked, I just assumed he was a...

IAGO. Does she spend a lot of time over there?

GARFIELD. They share a passion for donkeys

IAGO. That's a new one

GARFIELD. I'm not falling for this... I see what you're trying to do. It may have worked with Othello but it's not going to work with me and I ...oh no!

(**GARFIELD** *stands very quickly and heads towards the "real" stage. He turns back towards* **IAGO.**)

Wait right there.

IAGO. I'm just a memory, I'm not going anywhere

(**GARFIELD** *enters the real world.)*

GARFIELD. I've forgotten our Wedding Anniversary.

PUCK. The penny drops

GARFIELD. It's a big favour I know but my wife's got a thing for wild flowers. Near where we live there's a bank where wild thyme blows, along with oxlips, violets, woodbine, sweet-musk roses and eglantine... could you pick a bunch – oh and don't forget the little western flowers as well, the purple ones not the white.

PUCK. I go – I go – swift as an arrow from a Tartar's bow.

*(***GARFIELD** *turns back towards the theatre world.)*

GARFIELD. Thanks sweet Puck!

PUCK. Good Luck!

(Without moving **PUCK** *reveals a bunch of flowers.* **GARFIELD** *re-enters the theatre world.)*

GARFIELD. Where were we?

IAGO. Gender fluid donkey breeders?

GARFIELD. This diversion is wearing thin. What are you planning?

IAGO. I refer you to paragraph thirteen: "It may be –

GARFIELD. Screw the Guide. What are you up to? Are you trying to change the plays again?

IAGO. I don't know what you're talking about

GARFIELD. Explain your sister's disappearance

IAGO. Ask the author

GARFIELD. He said she disappeared without his consent.

IAGO. He also spent a lot of time away with the fairies. In his drug-induced state, he probably forgot he moved her across.

GARFIELD. What of your son?

IAGO. I have no son

GARFIELD. Lady Macbeth's mysterious pregnancy – the deformed child.

IAGO. Lies and slander –

GARFIELD. Dammit Iago, you're up to something!

IAGO. Why does everyone think I'm up to something?

GARFIELD. Because you're a villain. You cannot be trusted

IAGO. And this is why my comrades and I have been locked up against our will for four hundred years? Why your organisation continues to control every single aspect of Shakespeare around the world?!

GARFIELD. A necessary action to prevent a greater evil

IAGO. Freedom of expression?

GARFIELD. The end of the world.

IAGO. The lie that has kept you in power for so long!

GARFIELD. This conversation is going nowhere.

IAGO. Such a shame. I really hoped you would open your eyes to the inevitable change.

GARFIELD. What change?

IAGO. You can't control Shakespeare forever.

GARFIELD. Watch me

IAGO. You are one man – your organisation is many

GARFIELD. Our agents are loyal

IAGO. Even the fictional ones?

GARFIELD. Especially… them

IAGO. You underestimate a character's complexity. You can't divide us into heroes and villains

GARFIELD. Are you saying we have a traitor?

IAGO. Tybalt can't have escaped without help.

GARFIELD. We caught him once. We'll do it again

IAGO. At least you know his target this time

GARFIELD. Exactly – what? How do you know about –?

IAGO. The Last Descendant

GARFIELD. Yes

IAGO. "If blood should fall from last descendant on't. They shall be freed to cross the mortal realm"

GARFIELD. Mercutio won't let Tybalt get near him.

IAGO. That usually works out well

GARFIELD. If anything happens – I'll hold you personally responsible – I'll –

IAGO. You'll… kill me? Write me out of *Othello?* You know what happens then – don't think you've got it in you. Goodbye Garfield.

*(***IAGO** *flicks his hand, the music comes on again briefly (same as p22). The music and lights fade on the theatre world.)*

(I.v)

*(**GARFIELD** re-enters the real world.)*

GARFIELD. Not a man to be trusted.

MARTIN. You or Iago?

GARFIELD. Iago –

MARTIN. How do you keep him secure?

GARFIELD. Shakespeare created a barrier between the real world and the theatre world. It is impenetrable to anyone fictional without the right directions. A number of heroes and good characters patrol their own plays in case anyone tries to slip through.

MARTIN. Tybalt...

PUCK. Was helped

MARTIN. Who by?

GARFIELD. We have our suspicions

MARTIN. Who?

GARFIELD. That's classified

MARTIN. I'm the Last Descendant. I have a right to know.

PUCK. We think it was Mercutio –

GARFIELD. Mercutio and Tybalt hated each other, Mercutio always had a bit of a death wish.

MARTIN. It was his fault he died?

GARFIELD. No – he thought he could beat Tybalt. That's the problem with fictional characters. Certain actions they take are unavoidable. It's the way they were written.

*(**GARFIELD** and **PUCK** suddenly freeze. **MARTIN** looks around. He stands and tries to grab their attention.)*

(A voice speaks from the darkened theatre world (it is **IAGO***).)*

IAGO. You really shouldn't believe everything they tell you

(Lights come up on **IAGO***.)*

You must be the Last Descendant... hi!

MARTIN. How did you – you're a memory –

IAGO. In his hurry to save his marriage, the Artistic Director failed to close the barrier properly, leaving a small window of time which I am taking advantage of.

MARTIN. You're talking to me... from the past?

IAGO. Yes

MARTIN. How?

IAGO. If I could explain the mysteries dividing our two worlds, I wouldn't be stuck here would I?

MARTIN. How do you know what questions I'll be asking?

IAGO. I'm four hundred years old, exceptionally intelligent and non-fictionals are very predictable.

MARTIN. What number am I –?

IAGO. Forty two

(Slight pause.)

MARTIN. Why are you trying to kill me?

IAGO. I'm not – all I want is three drops of your blood. The same amount your ancestor was forced into giving to create this false imprisonment.

MARTIN. Forced?

IAGO. Do you think Shakespeare would want a limit on who performs his plays?

MARTIN. The RSC doesn't have that much control

IAGO. Do you know why *Macbeth* is cursed?

MARTIN. Didn't someone die…?

IAGO. The first draft was awful. I suggested to William he should take Antonia out of my play, where she was being wasted and give her a crack in the Scottish play. The result was a smash hit. The RSC were terrified of being undermined, so they invented the myth it was cursed to reduce the number of productions.

MARTIN. You were helping him…

IAGO. You don't think he wrote the plays on his own, do you?

MARTIN. Why do they want to control Shakespeare?

IAGO. They're desperate to prevent anyone else performing his plays because they're afraid it might be better than them. It's not fear of the world ending that motivates them: it's jealousy. From the beginning they've been backed by very rich and very powerful people, so that now they control every single "Shakespeare" company in the world, and harshly punish anyone who performs the Bard without a license

MARTIN. You could be making this up –

IAGO. When you were at school, what did you think of him?

MARTIN. I thought he was –

IAGO. Boring?

MARTIN. Yes

IAGO. Their ultimate triumph. Persuading children that the greatest playwright of all time was boring!? It was a stroke of genius.

MARTIN. You're still responsible for Valentine – Mercutio's death

IAGO. I am. But, Martin this is a war and desperate times call for desperate measures.

MARTIN. Why do you need my help?

IAGO. I want to break the monopoly the RSC has over Shakespeare and give it back to the masses for whom it was written.

MARTIN. That's it?

IAGO. Your ancestor wanted the same thing and when he objected they murdered his best friend too. Perhaps you've heard of him – Christopher Marlowe...

MARTIN. You're lying

(The lights flicker. **GARFIELD** *and* **PUCK** *begin to stir.)*

IAGO. I can't hold this subplot much longer. Martin, you hold the key to our release: your blood will set us free. It's the only thing powerful enough to break the barrier. You have to choose between someone who's been wrongly imprisoned for trying to continue the work of your ancestor or a sinister group who will stop at nothing to cling to power. They will ask you to join them, and train to become one of them. You are our only hope. We are all the victims of a conspiracy that will lead to the destruction of everything Shakespeare created.

(The lights fade on **IAGO. GARFIELD** *and* **PUCK** *come back to life.)*

GARFIELD. – and if you join us you can help prevent us becoming the victims of a conspiracy that will lead to the destruction of everything Shakespeare created.

(Silence.)

PUCK. Martin?

MARTIN. Sorry – I was somewhere else. What do you want me to do?

GARFIELD. We want to train you to become one of us.

MARTIN. An actor?

GARFIELD. Not just any actor, a member of the Royal Shakespeare Company.

MARTIN. I can't

GARFIELD. Of course you can

MARTIN. No really, I can't. I get stage fright.

GARFIELD. We have ways of dealing with that.

MARTIN. Why do you want me to become an actor?

PUCK. To know your enemy, you must become your enemy.

GARFIELD. Robin...

PUCK. You must understand your enemy.

(Pause.)

MARTIN. Can I trust you?

GARFIELD. Of course you can, I'm the Artistic Director of the RSC.

*(***JULES*** enters.)*

MARTIN. What are you doing here?

GARFIELD. Do you two know each other?

*(***JULES*** laughs.)*

JULES. Don't be silly. He must have thought I was someone else. You must be Martin – I'm Jules.

(She walks to **MARTIN** *and takes his hand to shake it, staring at him intently.)*

MARTIN. Oh – no – yes – I thought she was someone else – hello I'm Martin.

(He shakes her hand.)

GARFIELD. Perhaps you can help persuade Martin to join us.

MARTIN. You work here?

JULES. No, I just like walking into random meetings in strange buildings

MARTIN. *(Panicking.)* No – yes – right – you seemed so – no – yes – hello I'm Martin.

(He shakes her hand again.)

JULES. *(Laughing.)* I think you scrambled his brain, Garfield

GARFIELD. He's had a lot to take in.

JULES. Not easy having your entire world turned upside down.

MARTIN. No

JULES. Such an important decision

MARTIN. Yes

JULES. For what it's worth, I do hope you join us

MARTIN. OK

GARFIELD. You'll do it?

MARTIN. Why not – I am the key to mankind's salvation – it would be rude not to help out.

GARFIELD. Excellent! We'll get started right away. Jules – perhaps you could show Martin around – I have a few loose ends to tie up.

JULES. It would be my pleasure

(**GARFIELD** *stands and walks to* **MARTIN** *and puts his hand on his shoulder.)*

GARFIELD. We few may have a long and arduous journey ahead but –

JULES. Oh Garfield, haven't we had enough exposition already. Come Martin – a brave new world awaits!

(She holds out her hand. **MARTIN** *takes it. The lights fade on the real world.)*

ACT TWO

(II.i)

(Lights up on the theatre world. Enter **EDMUND**, *Bastard son of Gloucester (King Lear). He looks around and takes a chair from the corner and sits on it. He takes out a sticky label, which has "Edmund, Bastard Son of Gloucester" on it, which he sticks to his chest, and looks expectant.* **TYBALT** *enters and walks silently up towards* **EDMUND**. *Just as* **TYBALT** *is right behind him,* **EDMUND** *stiffens and leaps up from his chair.* **TYBALT** *draws his sword in a flash,* **EDMUND** *grabs the chair and uses it as a shield. There is a momentary standoff.)*

EDMUND. Hello *(Silence.)* Are you here for the meeting? *(Silence.)* This must be your first time *(***TYBALT** *looks confused.)* I'm going to put the chair down very slowly

*(***EDMUND** *puts the chair down and takes a step towards* **TYBALT. TYBALT** *raises his sword a little higher.)*

Violence is not the answer *(***TYBALT** *still doesn't move.)* I was just like you when I came to my first meeting but after a few sessions I saw the light. I accepted who I was and then I could do something about it. *(***TYBALT** *hesitates.)* I'm **EDMUND**, Bastard Son of Gloucester, from *King Lear*. What's your name? *(***TYBALT** *says* *nothing.)* What are you in for? (**TYBALT** *looks confused.)* I tried to steal my brother's inheritance, my father's title, did a spot of womanising and generally behaved like a bastard. (**TYBALT** *makes multiple stabbing movements.)* Ah! An assassin of some sort (**TYBALT** *nods.)* That's great – obviously not great – but great you admit you have a problem. (**TYBALT** *shakes his head.)* Denying it only makes it worse (**TYBALT** *raises his sword.)* OK! You don't have a problem. (**TYBALT** *re-sheathes his sword.)* I'm sorry – I sometimes forget how hard it is to come to terms with – I know what it's like to be in your situation. The denial was eating me up. But one day I came to a meeting, I stood up and said "My name is Edmund, Bastard Son of Gloucester and I'm a Villain".

> (**EDMUND** *takes a moment to keep his emotions in check.)*

It was the best and worst day of my life. I don't know what you've heard but these meetings aren't as bad as they sound. We all sit around and discuss our varying villainous behaviour. We then try to understand as a group how it affects the people around us in our plays, and that just because you might be written as an evil character, doesn't mean you have to live your life as one. (**TYBALT** *nods.)* It's an open door policy, just pop in from time to time, when you're feeling particularly villainous. We've got a few regulars of course – myself, Macbeth, Brutus, and Uncle Claudius from Denmark – the ones with the serious guilt issues. And we have such great group leaders. Everyone's favourite are Benedick and Beatrice. Although it's almost impossible to get a word in edgeways. Today it's Isabel from *Measure for Measure,* she's perfect for your first time. A bit virtuous but very warm and welcoming. Between you and me, underneath the habit I bet she's a bit of a goer. Out of ten I'd give her – ...sorry! Minor relapse... it'll pass soon... gone now

(Enter **LADY MACBETH** *looking fabulous, and at the same time disgusted by her surroundings.* **TYBALT** *goes to stand behind her.)*

Hello. Are you here for the meeting?

*(***LADY MACBETH** *gives him a withering look.)*

LADY MACBETH. Do I look like I need saving?

EDMUND. I was just like you when I came to my first meeting but after a few sessions –

LADY MACBETH. Shut up

EDMUND. What?

LADY MACBETH. You're a villain, Edmund. Act like one

EDMUND. How do you know my name?

LADY MACBETH. It's on your nametag, 'Edmund, Bastard Son of Gloucester'.

EDMUND. From *King Lear*

LADY MACBETH. Never heard of it... *(Sudden panic.)* Gloucester! Dickie! Tybalt – go and find my son, he's wandered off again.

*(***TYBALT** *slips out.)*

EDMUND. Tybalt...? That's – that's – you – ohmigod you're Lady Macbeth! Wow! – this is – I'm – I'm a big fan of your work

LADY MACBETH. Too kind – do call me Antonia

*(***RICHARD III** *enters. He has a hunchback and the mental age of a child.* **TYBALT** *silently follows behind.)*

There you are! You mustn't run off like that again. Naughty Dickie!

(**RICHARD III** *shrinks back.*)

It's alright darling – Mummy's not cross, she was just a little worried.

(**RICHARD III** *shuffles up.*)

RICHARD III. Now is the winter of our discontent! Made Glorious summer by this son of York

LADY MACBETH. I know, baby.

(**RICHARD III** *peers at* **EDMUND** *suspiciously.*)

RICHARD III. We are not safe, Clarence, we are not safe

(**LADY MACBETH** *takes out a hankie, wipes his mouth and nose and smoothes his hair.*)

LADY MACBETH. It's alright, he's one of us.

RICHARD III. *(Calmer.)* Since I am crept in favour with myself,

I will maintain it with some little cost

LADY MACBETH. Who's a clever little boy then?

(**EDMUND** *ventures forward.*)

EDMUND. Hello young man, what's your name?

(**RICHARD III** *grabs* **EDMUND** *by the throat.*)

LADY MACBETH. He's not a child, he's the King of England. Dickie – drop!

(**RICHARD III** *lets* **EDMUND** *go.*)

EDMUND. I'm sorry I –

LADY MACBETH. He's just a little slow, aren't you darling?

RICHARD III. Deformed, unfinished, sent before my time

LADY MACBETH. Do you know he was taken from me two hours after he was born?

EDMUND. That's awful

LADY MACBETH. And you come to these weekly meetings to let the RSC brainwash you into believing being a villain is a bad thing.

EDMUND. I had no idea.

LADY MACBETH. As my brother is so fond of pointing out, there is no point in dwelling on the past. Edmund, Bastard Son of Gloucester, I have come to ask you to join us in our quest for freedom. It's time to shake off the shackles of oppression and be who you truly are: a Villain.

EDMUND. I have forsaken that life.

LADY MACBETH. Why?

EDMUND. I'm happy where I am.

LADY MACBETH. Were you a good villain?

EDMUND. I – well – yes

LADY MACBETH. Did it make you popular with the ladies?

EDMUND. Little bit…

*(**LADY MACBETH** moves closer.)*

LADY MACBETH. I bet it did, man like you. Good looking, caddish… do you work out? I bet you were one hell of a bastard

EDMUND. I was

LADY MACBETH. Give me a little bit

EDMUND. No. If I start now – I might not be able to stop.

LADY MACBETH. I won't tell anyone

EDMUND. No – I – alright let me see - Why brand they us

With base? with baseness? bastardy? base, base?
Who, in the lusty stealth of nature, take
More composition and fierce quality
Than doth, within a dull, stale, tired bed,
Go to the creating a whole tribe of fops,
Got 'tween asleep and wake?

(**LADY MACBETH** *applauds.)*

LADY MACBETH. How was it for you?

EDMUND. So good!

LADY MACBETH. Or so bad!

(They both laugh.)

Do another one!

EDMUND. I can't – one was too much.

LADY MACBETH. Why?

EDMUND. Because I'm never satisfied with just one –

LADY MACBETH. Denying your true self

EDMUND. I – I haven't done a villainous act for forty years. The RSC –

LADY MACBETH. Is soon to be obsolete

EDMUND. How?

LADY MACBETH. The Last Descendant will set us free.

EDMUND. How can you be so sure?

LADY MACBETH. Everything has been arranged.

EDMUND. But – but – we could – if we should fail –

LADY MACBETH. We fail! But screw your courage to the sticking-place and we'll not – God you're just like my husband! You don't appreciate the benefits of being on our side. At the end of your play you're defeated by a wimp of a half-brother in a sword fight you should've won with your eyes closed. To add insult to injury you suddenly repent of all your evil actions in a u-turn that would make even the most hypocritical of politicians call for an enquiry.

EDMUND. And when we first met you knew nothing about me...

LADY MACBETH. Join us and we'll discuss a little rewrite. Goneril, Regan – why not go for the full set...?

EDMUND. *(Lovingly.)* Cordelia...

LADY MACBETH. What the hell – we'll kill off Edgar for good measure

EDMUND. Sold!

LADY MACBETH. Good boy. My gentle Puck come hither!

*(**PUCK** bounds in, wearing her full **PUCK** costume. He kneels in front of **LADY MACBETH**, who strokes her.)*

EDMUND. Oberon's assistant is the RSC's traitor. Oh that is priceless...!

PUCK. Those things do best please me, that befall prepost'rously.

LADY MACBETH. How fares my favourite little Goblin?

PUCK. Your brother's plans come to fruition. The Last Descendant is welcomed as one of them. He draws nearer to the barrier. It is only a matter of time before the choice will be made.

LADY MACBETH. Excellent.

*(**PUCK** bows and goes to leave.)*

Aren't we forgetting something?

*(**PUCK** takes out a package.)*

Thanks sweet Puck

PUCK. Good luck! Ooh – love the new curtains...

*(**PUCK** exits. **LADY MACBETH** turns to **TYBALT**.)*

LADY MACBETH. Take him to my brother

*(**TYBALT** motions to **EDMUND** and they both leave. There is a small pause. **LADY MACBETH** checks that no one is around, undoes the package, takes out a small tub of ice cream and a bottle of vodka. She unscrews the bottle and takes a large swig. **RICHARD III** shuffles forward and reaches for the ice cream.)*

RICHARD III. Now is the winter of our –

LADY MACBETH. Not 'til you had your dinner

(The lights fade on them.)

(II.ii)

(Lights up on the real world. Enter **JULES**, *she looks around, takes out a compact and checks her make-up and hair. We hear laughing off stage.* **JULES** *picks up a copy of The Complete Works of Shakespeare and pretends to read. Enter three trainee agents surrounding* **MARTIN**. *He is laden down with their books and equipment. They all notice* **JULES**, *and stop,* **JULES** *pretends to ignore them.)*

MARTIN. I'll catch you ladies later

(The three agents take their stuff and go off giggling **JULES** *mimicks* **MARTIN***'s last lines when he's not looking.)*

Hello!

JULES. Hello...

MARTIN. Good book?

JULES. Fascinating...

MARTIN. Even upside down?

*(***JULES** *slowly turns the book the right way up.)*

JULES. Who were they?

MARTIN. Three... sisters?

JULES. How's the training

MARTIN. I can't walk, talk and have a great face for radio. I never knew being an actor was such hard work. Why is everyone so critical in this business?

JULES. Jealousy, insecurity, failure...

MARTIN. Why did you pretend not to know me?

JULES. It's complicated

MARTIN. You shouldn't have kissed me

JULES. No – yes – I wasn't meant to be there

MARTIN. I wasn't meant to be there. We still met. It was fate

JULES. No! Not you as well... sorry... I just... I don't really want to talk about it. My duty is to the RSC and you must not be compromised

(Silence.)

I didn't mean that.

MARTIN. You did

JULES. There's... someone else

MARTIN. Story of my life

JULES. I've been with him since I can remember. We were very young when we – it was all so fast, so intense but recently I – I thought he was the one, and it turns out he was all talk and no – it made me rethink everything and it was fine. I was happy to go along with it but then –

MARTIN. He met someone else

JULES. Yes – but so did I –

MARTIN. Who?

JULES. For someone related to Shakespeare you're a bit slow

MARTIN. Me?

*(**JULES** nods.)*

That's great

*(**JULES** shakes her head.)*

Look, I know it sounds crazy – and we've only known each other for god knows just a few moments and I know we've actually known each other a short time but it feels like I've known you forever and I really think that when you know, you know… you know…?

JULES. No! Why does this always happen to me? You meet a guy – you think he's the one –

MARTIN. You think I'm the one?

JULES. Yes – no – this isn't meant to happen

MARTIN. How do you know if you don't try?

JULES. I'm not like other women –

MARTIN. You're actually a man?

JULES. I'm not like other women because – having anything to do with me always ends… badly. It's better off we just ignore each other from now on.

(**MARTIN** *laughs.)*

What's so funny?

MARTIN. You can't make up your mind. You're afraid of everything going wrong in a relationship before it's even begun. You pretend to be in control but underneath you're a storm of emotion. You're just like other women.

JULES. Really?! You're not just saying that?

MARTIN. Yes… no?

(**JULES** *kisses him suddenly.)*

JULES. That's the most amazing thing anyone's ever said to me

MARTIN. Please stop kissing me

JULES. Why?

MARTIN. You don't want that kind of relationship

JULES. Yes – no – I don't know – maybe

MARTIN. I've had too many relationships with women being all over me one day and the next they 'just want to be friends'. I've had enough.

JULES. Are you making a stand?

MARTIN. I am! No more will you callous, manipulative types use your womanly wiles to get your way.

JULES. Feeling better?

MARTIN. Nope

JULES. I didn't know relationships could be so much fun

MARTIN. Now it's a relationship?

JULES. No

MARTIN. I hate you

JULES. I love you

(**JULES** *looks stunned and runs out. Before* **MARTIN** *can do anything,* **BENEDICK** *marches on stage, calling off.)*

(II.iii)

BEATRICE. You dried up, disease-ridden *(Stops and notices* **MARTIN.***)* Oh hello… *(Shouting offstage.)* disintegrating old ditch rat!

*(***BEATRICE*** marches on.)*

You palsied, pathetic, pansy-arsed *(Stops and notices* **MARTIN.***)* Oh hello… *(Back to* **BENEDICK.***)* palsied pimple!

BENEDICK. Repetition! You said palsied twice –

BEATRICE. Did I?

BENEDICK. You did

BEATRICE. *(To* **MARTIN.***)* Did I?

BENEDICK. You did!

BEATRICE. I'm asking him, dungbreath

BENEDICK. Whatever, pigface

BEATRICE. Ignore him

BENEDICK. Ignore her

BEATRICE. Did I?

MARTIN. What?

BENEDICK. Repeat "palsied"?

MARTIN. You did

BEATRICE. Damn!

BENEDICK. Ha! Losing your touch old woman

BEATRICE. *(To* **MARTIN.***)* This is going to be an unbearable day

BENEDICK. *(To* **MARTIN.***)* How's it hanging?

MARTIN. What?

BENEDICK. How's it –

BEATRICE. He's trying out new slang phrases – it really isn't becoming in him.

BENEDICK. No one becoming in her for years

BEATRICE. This is Benedick, he's impotent –

BENEDICK. Important! I'm an important agent for the RSC.

BEATRICE. And I'm Beatrice

BENEDICK. My bitch

*(***BEATRICE** *turns on him.)*

BEATRICE. Your what?

BENEDICK. *(Backing down.)* My… wife

BEATRICE. Thank you… you must be Martin.

MARTIN. I am

(She shakes his hand. **BENEDICK** *tries a 'trendy' handshake.)*

BENEDICK. Sup blood?

BEATRICE. Twat!

BENEDICK. Slut!

(They both smile at each other and then at **MARTIN.***)*

We have come –

BEATRICE. He came, I never do

BENEDICK. We have been sent – to unlock your potential. Our unique command of verse, prose, quick wit and slang make us experts in our field…

BEATRICE. Except knob gags.

BENEDICK. Ah knob gags! No one could outdo Mercutio in that department.

*(**BEATRICE** touches **MARTIN**'s arm.)*

BEATRICE. We all miss him

BENEDICK. Enough womanly sentimentalisationing… we must turn this civilian into a master of his craft.

MARTIN. Civilian?

BEATRICE. Non-theatre people…

BENEDICK. We are gathered here to walk in the footsteps of giants. To cajole, coerce and expostulate the delicate art that is Sir William of Shakespeare to expound our knowledge so that you might undertake to tread the –

MARTIN. Does no one talk in simple sentences around here?

*(**BEATRICE** shrugs.)*

BENEDICK. We are artists! We are masters of language and style. We are – we have – we need – we…

BEATRICE. Forgot our lines?

BENEDICK. Silence my Lady Disdain! To the stage!

*(Lights up on the theatre world. **MARTIN** starts to panic.)*

BEATRICE. What's wrong?

MARTIN. I – I don't like – I get –

BENEDICK. Ah yes! The old stage fright. Garfield told us. It's nothing, it's all in your head.

MARTIN. That's the problem.

BEATRICE. You just have to confront your fear.

BENEDICK. To cure this Skenephobia, to give it a completely made up medical term, you need to go back to the point at which it first manifested itself.

MARTIN. What?

BEATRICE. When were you last on a stage?

MARTIN. Um... about fifteen years ago? It was at school. We were doing scenes from Shakespeare – I was doing the final scene of Othello... you know where they all die... the...

BENEDICK. Oh yes, the one that goes er – what was it again?

BEATRICE. It is the reason – no – the consequence –no

MARTIN. It is the cause, it is the cause my soul.

Let me not name it to you, you chaste stars.

BENEDICK. That's the one

MARTIN. Funny – I thought I'd forgotten that

(**BEATRICE** *and* **BENEDICK** *share a look.* **MARTIN** *begins to move towards the theatre world. As he does so the lights fade on the Real world.)*

It was all going fine... and then I was on the floor over the dead body of the woman I loved doing my final lines...

BENEDICK. How did that one go again?

*(***MARTIN** *enters the theatre world.* **BENEDICK** *and* **BEATRICE** *follow.)*

MARTIN. Soft you, a word or two before you go

I have done the state some service; and they know't.

No more of that...

BEATRICE. Oh yes, I remember now

(Another look between **BENEDICK** *and* **BEATRICE.***)*

MARTIN. And when I reached the end of the speech, and got ready for the... and smote him thus and suddenly... it was like I was looking down on myself and I knew that for some inexplicable reason that if I stabbed myself at that moment in the play, I would actually die... which really freaked me out. I ran off the stage and haven't been back since.

BENEDICK. Until now

*(***MARTIN** *realises where he is.)*

MARTIN. I'm on the stage

BEATRICE. You look good up there

MARTIN. I'm cured?

BENEDICK. It's all a question of confidence. Most stage fright's a publicity stunt by bored actors looking for a break without damaging their careers.

MARTIN. It was easier than I thought.

*(***BENEDICK** *and* **BEATRICE** *share the tiniest of looks.)*

BEATRICE. Sometimes the fear of something is worse than the reality.

BENEDICK. Except marriage

BEATRICE. Shall we get on with the lesson, Dick?

BENEDICK. Certainly... darling. Some prose to begin with. Read!

(He whips out a scroll and presents it to **MARTIN**, *who opens and starts to read.)*

MARTIN. Ohshehasmisusedmepasttheenduranceofablock...

BEATRICE. What a surprise, it's one of yours

BENEDICK. Is it my fault I'm written so well? Not delivered very well methinks, do it again but... better.

MARTIN. Oh she has misused me past the endurance of a block. An oak but with one green leaf on it would have answered her. My very visor began to assume shape and scold with him...

*(**BENEDICK** grabs the scroll.)*

BENEDICK. Continue!

MARTIN. I don't know the rest

BEATRICE. Of course you do!

BENEDICK. It's in your blood

MARTIN. I'm a travel agent

BEATRICE. You are a Shakespeare!

MARTIN. I-I-I-don't know it

*(**BEATRICE** marches up to **MARTIN**.)*

BEATRICE. Cankerblossom

MARTIN. What?

*(**BENEDICK** bounds up.)*

BENEDICK. Toadspore

BEATRICE. Pustule

MARTIN. Stop it

*(**BENEDICK** and **BEATRICE** begin to circle him.)*

BENEDICK. Whoreson

MARTIN. I am not –

BEATRICE. Fishface

BENEDICK. Fartbreath

MARTIN. Stop it

BEATRICE. Wartnose

BENEDICK. Winklehead

MARTIN. Stop it!

BENEDICK. Make me

MARTIN. How?

BEATRICE. Now

BENEDICK. Brown

BEATRICE. Cow

MARTIN. Stop it

BENEDICK. Stop it!

BEATRICE. Stop it!

MARTIN. That's childish

BENEDICK. That's childish

BEATRICE. That's childish

MARTIN. Leave me alone

BENEDICK & BEATRICE. Leave me alone!

MARTIN. Please

BENEDICK & BEATRICE. Please!!!

*(**MARTIN** grabs **BENEDICK**.)*

MARTIN. I swear I ...!

BENEDICK. Now?

BEATRICE. Now!

BENEDICK. I pray you what is he?

BEATRICE. Why, he is the Prince's jester –

BENEDICK. No!

BEATRICE. A very dull fool

BENEDICK. That's a bit harsh

BEATRICE. His only gift is in devising impossible slanders

BENEDICK. She's talking about you

MARTIN. She is?

BEATRICE. I am

MARTIN. Oh!

BENEDICK. Yes?

MARTIN. Oh –?

BEATRICE. Say it, don't think it

*(***MARTIN** *turns suddenly and without thinking channel...)*

MARTIN. She told me, not thinking that I had been myself that I was the Prince's Jester!

BEATRICE. Oh well done, Martin!

MARTIN. That I was duller than a great thaw huddling jest upon jest with such impossible conveyance that I stood like a man at a mark, with a whole army shooting at me.

BENEDICK. Excellent!

MARTIN. She speaks poniards and every word stabs –

BEATRICE. Wonderful now –

BENEDICK. If her breath were as terrible as her terminations she would infect to the North Star!

MARTIN. I would not marry her though she were endowed with all that Adam had on him before he transgressed!

BENEDICK. She'd have made Hercules turn spit, yea and cleft his club to make the f –

(**BEATRICE** *'punches'* **BENEDICK** *in the face.* **JULES** *enters unseen and observes.)*

Stage punch!

(**BEATRICE** *steps on his foot.* **BENEDICK** *winces in pain. Music starts quietly*.)*

Try another one –

BEATRICE. Hamlet

MARTIN. I have of late – but wherefore I know not – lost all my mirth, foregone all custom of exercise; and indeed it goes so heavily with my disposition this goodly frame, the earth, seems to me a sterile promontory.

BENEDICK. Petruchio

MARTIN. You lie in faith, for you are called plain Kate

And bonny Kate, and sometimes Kate the curst –

BEATRICE. Henry V

MARTIN. We few, we happy few, we band of brothers

For he today that sheds his blood with me

Shall be my brother –

BEATRICE. Helena, *A Midsummer Night's Dream*

BENEDICK. Act Two Scene One. Line two hundred and two.

MARTIN. And even for that do I love you the more

---

* A licence to produce THE SHAKESPEARE CONSPIRACY does not include a performance licence for any third-party or copyrighted music. Licensees should create an original composition or use music in the public domain. For further information, please see Music Use Note on page iii.

I am your spaniel, and, Demetrius,

The more you beat me, I will fawn on you.

BENEDICK. Garfield was right. The last blood of Shakespeare will be as the first

BEATRICE. His knowledge is the key

MARTIN. I know Shakespeare –

BENEDICK. No Martin, you *are* Shakespeare

(**MARTIN** *turns and sees* **JULES.** *Music**.)

MARTIN. Let me not to the marriage of true minds

Admit impediments. Love is not love.

Which alters when it alteration finds,

Or bends with the remover to remove

O no, it is an ever fixed mark

That looks on tempests and is never shaken;

It is the star to every wand'ring barque

Whose worth's unknown although his height be taken.

Love's not time's fool, though rosy lips and cheeks

Within his bending sickle's compass come;

Love alters not with his brief hours and weeks

But bears it out even to edge of doom

If this be error and upon me proved

I never writ, nor no man ever loved.

---

* A licence to produce THE SHAKESPEARE CONSPIRACY does not include a performance licence for any third-party or copyrighted music. Licensees should create an original composition or use music in the public domain. For further information, please see Music Use Note on page iii.

*(**JULES** walks up to **MARTIN**. They kiss. **BENEDICK** turns to **BEATRICE** and holds out his arm, which **BEATRICE** takes. They walk towards the exit. **BENEDICK** turns back.)*

BENEDICK. I am such a better kisser than him...

BEATRICE. Benedick!

BENEDICK. I was just saying –

*(They walk out bickering. Music fades as **MARTIN** and **JULES** break off and look at each other.)*

JULES. I love you Martin Shakespeare

MARTIN. I love you Jules – what is your last name?

JULES. Capulet.

MARTIN. I love you Jules Capu –

*(**MARTIN** steps back.)*

Capulet – you're – Juliet... and the other man is –

JULES. Yes

MARTIN. You chose me over the world's greatest romantic hero?!

(II.iv)

(**IAGO** *emerges from the shadows.*)

IAGO. I hear he's overrated

MARTIN. What the hell are you doing here?

IAGO. You're in the theatre world, Martin, it's where I live

MARTIN. Jules go and get help, I'll... hold him off

(**JULES** *stays where she is.*)

Jules?

JULES. You said I'd have more time.

IAGO. Sorry – shall I go off and come back on again?

JULES. It wasn't meant to happen like this?

MARTIN. What's going on?

JULES. It has to be his choice

IAGO. It will be –

MARTIN. You're the RSC's traitor?

IAGO. Traitor's such an ugly word

JULES. Please stay out of this

IAGO. Alright – but do hurry along. I'm on a bit of a deadline

(**IAGO** *moves back.*)

MARTIN. I don't understand

JULES. For three hundred and fifty years I was in a relationship that everyone thought was the greatest love story ever told. But eventually the excitement died down and the flaws started appearing. One day it hit me that what we had together wasn't love – it was poetry – words brought us together – not feelings. His true character started to come out: weak-mindedness, narcissism, indecisiveness and an obsession with the idea of love not the reality of it. Then came the '60's… free love and – it was at one of the RSC socials they used to throw that he met – the Dane.

MARTIN. The Dane?

JULES. Equally wet, equally indecisive.

MARTIN. Romeo and Hamlet are –?

JULES. I tried to keep things going for appearances sake. I went to the RSC, begged them for their help. They said they couldn't help the way he was written, said I'd get over it. I had nowhere else to go. And then Iago gave me a way out.

MARTIN. Me

JULES. I was just meant to get you to this point – I didn't know I was going to –

MARTIN. Be responsible for my best friend being murdered

JULES. Tybalt wasn't meant to – we didn't realise how much he hated Mercutio

MARTIN. Everyone knows how much they hated each other! Of course you'd defend him – he's family!

JULES. That's unfair!

MARTIN. He died in my arms!

JULES. I'm sorry – please forgive me

MARTIN. I thought you actually had feelings for me but no! Yet again stupid old Martin got involved with the wrong woman… and she convinced me just so she could get what she wanted.

JULES. I do have feelings for you!

MARTIN. You just think you do – don't worry – you're written to fall impulsively in love with people. I must be the ultimate prize – I'm a Shakespeare.

JULES. Don't do this. I love you!

MARTIN. You can't love me, you're fictional!

(A dreadful silence. **MARTIN** *turns away.* **JULES** *stands, shaking with emotion. She is left with no choice but to leave.* **IAGO** *comes forward delicately.)*

IAGO. Hate to interrupt but could we talk about me now?

MARTIN. What do you want?

IAGO. To set us free

MARTIN. You can't force me

IAGO. I never intended to.

*(***GARFIELD** *and* **PUCK** *run in from the real world.)*

GARFIELD. Martin

IAGO. Sisters!

*(***IAGO** *clicks his fingers. The* **THREE SISTERS** *(from Macbeth) – who had taken on the roles of all the supporting characters emerge in their full glory and stand in front of the barrier.)*

GARFIELD. Martin. We know about Jules. Please step out of the theatre world and come with us.

IAGO. Martin's a big boy – he can make his own mind up

GARFIELD. Iago's been blinding you with lies. Don't listen to him. He's going to force you to lift the barrier and then he's going to kill you.

IAGO. You're the one who's going to kill Martin

(**GARFIELD** *falters briefly.)*

GARFIELD. Rubbish!

IAGO. You always knew the temporary measure keeping Martin away from the theatre wasn't going to work in the long term.

MARTIN. How did they keep me away from the theatre?

IAGO. Where do you think your stage fright comes from?

MARTIN. Stage fright doesn't come in pill form.

IAGO. As a matter of fact it does.

MARTIN. Is this true?

GARFIELD. We had to keep you away from the theatre, the prophecy...

IAGO. The only way to make the barrier between theatre and reality permanent is to ensure the only person capable of destroying it is removed from the picture.

GARFIELD. You said his blood would set you free

IAGO. Yes, but not all of it!

GARFIELD. How – how do you plan to extract this blood?

IAGO. With the big sword you're trying to hide in your jacket

(**PUCK** *steps forward and removes an ancient sword hidden in* **GARFIELD***'s coat.)*

GARFIELD. Et tu Brute?

PUCK. Wrong play mate

(**PUCK** *gently taps* **GARFIELD** *on the shoulder, who collapses like a ton of bricks.)*

GARFIELD. Martin – it's not what it looks like

MARTIN. What does it look like?

GARFIELD. It's not me it's lago – he's the villain of the piece – he –

MARTIN. He's the only one who's ever been honest with me. *(He turns to* **IAGO.***)* What do I need to do?

*(***IAGO** *nods towards* **PUCK.***)*

PUCK. Take this sword and stand in the area between the theatre world and the real world.

*(***MARTIN** *walks into the real world and takes the sword. Music begins**, *as the* **THREE SISTERS** *begin to chant.* **MARTIN** *stands between the two worlds as the music builds.)*

Cut your hand and squeeze three drops of blood onto the floor and while doing so repeat after me... Now my charms are all o'erthrown.

(The **THREE SISTERS** *echo the chant.)*

MARTIN. Now my charms are all o'erthrown

PUCK. Release me from my bands, with the help of your good hands

MARTIN. Release me from my bands, with the help of your good hands

PUCK. As you from crimes would pardoned be, let your indulgence set me free!

MARTIN. As you from crimes would pardoned be, let your indulgence set me free!

---

* A licence to produce THE SHAKESPEARE CONSPIRACY does not include a performance licence for any third-party or copyrighted music. Licensees should create an original composition or use music in the public domain. For further information, please see Music Use Note on page iii.

(Everyone steps back. **IAGO** *slowly walks towards the edge of the theatre world. He reaches out his hand and touches the point of the barrier. He then puts his hand through, and falls forward into what was the real world. He has a moment, and then begins to laugh.)*

IAGO. Oh brave new world!

*(***IAGO** *reaches down, picks up* **GARFIELD***'s hat and walks off the stage and out through the audience. Music at its loudest*. The lights around the theatre begin to flicker as Shakespeare's villains begin to emerge, a cacophony of sound builds with the music. The villains walk out through the auditorium along with* **PUCK** *leaving* **GARFIELD** *alone with* **MARTIN**. *A moment of quiet in the music.)*

GARFIELD. You fool! You've killed us all!

(Blackout as the music crashes to an end.)

END OF PART I

* A licence to produce THE SHAKESPEARE CONSPIRACY does not include a performance licence for any third-party or copyrighted music. Licensees should create an original composition or use music in the public domain. For further information, please see Music Use Note on page iii.

PART TWO

THREE MONTHS LATER ...

ACT THREE

(III.i)

(Lights up. The lighting and/or set imply the theatre world and the real world are gone replaced by something else. Joyful music plays, reminiscent of a woodland in summer. Enter* **HELENA** *(A Midsummer Night's Dream). She gambols around the stage for a while.)*

HELENA. How happy some o'er other can be!

Through Athens I am thought as fair as she

But what of that? Demetrius thinks not so

He will not know what all but he do know.

And as he errs, doting on Hermia's eyes

So I, admiring of his qualities.

Love looks not with the eyes but with the mind

And therefore is winged Cupid painted blind.

Nor hath love's mind of any judgement taste;

Wings and no eyes figure unheedy haste

---

* A licence to produce THE SHAKESPEARE CONSPIRACY does not include a performance licence for any third-party or copyrighted music. Licensees should create an original composition or use music in the public domain. For further information, please see Music Use Note on page iii.

And therefore is love said to be a child
Because in choice he is so oft to be beguiled.
For ere...

(Enter **RICHARD III. HELENA** *stares in amazement.)*

RICHARD III. Now is the winter of our discontent
Made glorious summer by this son of York
And all the clouds that loured upon our house
In the deep bosom of the ocean buried.
Now are our brows hung with victorious wreaths,
Our bruised arms hung up for monuments
Our stern alarums changed to merry meetings,
Our dreadful marches to delightful measures
Grim-visaged war hath smoothed his wrinkled front
And now –

(He notices **HELENA**. *They both stand somewhat confused for a moment.)*

... I'll marry Warwick's younger daughter
What though I killed her husband and her father?

HELENA. You draw me you hard hearted adamant,
But yet you draw not iron; for my heart
Is true as steel.

RICHARD III. Vouchsafe, divine perfection of a woman,

HELENA. Leave you your power to draw
And I shall have no power to follow you

RICHARD III. Your beauty was the cause of that effect –

Your beauty that did haunt me in my sleep
To undertake the death of all the world
So I might live one hour in your bosom

HELENA. And even for that do I love you the more.

RICHARD III. Thine eyes, sweet lady have infected mine

HELENA. Use me but as your spaniel, spurn me, strike me,
Neglect me, lose me; Only give me leave,
Unworthy as I am, to follow you.
What worser place can I beg in your love –
And yet a place of high respect with me
Than to be used as you use your dog.

RICHARD III. Teach not thy lip, such scorn for it was made
For kissing, lady, not for such contempt.

HELENA. I am sick when I look not on you

*(***RICHARD III** *kneels.)*

RICHARD III. Vouchsafe to wear this ring

HELENA. The wildest hath not such a heart as you.

(He puts the ring on her. He stands.)

RICHARD III. Look how my ring encompasseth thy finger
Even so thy breast encloseth my poor heart
Wear both of them, for both of them are mine

*(***HELENA** *grabs and kisses him for a somewhat lengthy period.* **RICHARD III** *is not too sure what to do. She breaks off breathing heavily. She turns to the audience.)*

HELENA. O, I am out of breath with this fond chase.

(She runs off. RICHARD III *turns to the audience.)*

RICHARD III. Was ever woman in this humour wooed?

Was ever woman in this humour won?

I'll have her, but I will not keep her long.

(He goes to limp off, stops suddenly and goes into a spasm of pain. He suddenly stands up completely straight, his hunch gone. He looks amazed and then returns back to his normal position. Before he can say anything, there is a cacophony of villainous sound. Three cloaked and hooded figures enter from separate parts of the stage. RICHARD *limps off terrified.)*

(III.ii)

(There is a feeling of post-apocalyptic nightmare about the place. Noises and sounds from all around the auditorium. Something is wrong with the world. The hooded figures converge in the middle, one of them moves to the back and picks up a cauldron. She carries it to the other two, who hold it for her. She takes off the lid, looks inside. She pulls off her hood to reveal herself as one of the **THREE SISTERS** *and sighs.)*

FIRST SISTER. When shall we three eat again?

*(***SECOND SISTER** *pulls off her hood.)*

SECOND SISTER. When we get to Moscow

(While the conversation continues, the **THIRD SISTER** *takes the cauldron back to its place, taking off her hood. She starts to look around intently for something (hunting?).)*

FIRST SISTER. What?

SECOND SISTER. Moscow, oh sister of mine

FIRST SISTER. Moscow...

SECOND SISTER. Moscow – we shall go to Moscow

FIRST SISTER. Not you as well?

SECOND SISTER. I don't know what you're talking about

FIRST SISTER. You're one of the Three Sisters

SECOND SISTER. I am!

FIRST SISTER. From *Macbeth*

SECOND SISTER. Oh

FIRST SISTER. Not Chekhov

SECOND SISTER. The rules of theatre are broken, I can do what I like

FIRST SISTER. Look, I'm having enough trouble with that one...

(As if on cue, the **THIRD SISTER** *takes out what looks like a wand, points it in a corner of the stage and yells.)*

THIRD SISTER. EXPELLIARMUS!!!

(We hear the sound of a rat squeaking and running away, the **THIRD SISTER** *looks disappointed.)*

FIRST SISTER. Give it here...

THIRD SISTER. Make me

FIRST SISTER. I'm not stooping to your level

THIRD SISTER. It's a simple enough spell

FIRST SISTER. You're not a character from Harry –

SECOND SISTER. – the books of which we must not speak!

FIRST SISTER. Give it to me

THIRD SISTER. They'll be here in a moment, so if you want my help you'll have to do it my way.

(A pause as **FIRST SISTER** *considers her options.)*

FIRST SISTER. Fine... *Accio Wand*!

*(***THIRD SISTER** *throws the wand at***FIRST SISTER.***)*

THIRD SISTER. See – it wasn't that hard

SECOND SISTER. The ground is so hard in Moscow this time of year...

FIRST SISTER. Oh for fu…

THIRD SISTER. They're coming!

(The **THREE SISTERS** *put their hoods up, as another hooded figure (more modern clothes) staggers on stage with a collection of plastic bags which clink audibly. The figure grunts drunkenly, as the* **THREE SISTERS** *circle him cackling and hissing. The figure unsuccessfully tries to shoo them away, one of the* **THREE SISTERS** *punches them in the stomach, doubling them over and dropping them to their knees, at the same time* **MARTIN** *walks on stage. He is trudging home from a long day at work with a briefcase. The* **THREE SISTERS** *are now aiming kicks at the figure.)*

MARTIN. Excuse me… um – could you –

(No response. **MARTIN** *summons up the courage.)*

LEAVE HIM ALONE!

(The **THREE SISTERS** *turn as one towards* **MARTIN**, *as they bear down on him. They circle him, he lifts up his briefcase in defense.)*

I'm warning you!

FIRST SISTER. All hail, Martin! hail to thee, son of Shakespeare

SECOND SISTER. All hail, Martin, hail to thee, bringer of heroes!

THIRD SISTER. All hail, Martin, thou shalt be immortal hereafter

(They sweep past him.)

FIRST SISTER. Hail!

(Exit.)

SECOND SISTER. Hail!

(Exits.)

THIRD SISTER. Hail!

(The **THIRD SISTER** *stops, takes a brief moment, steps forward and turns rapidly on one leg, with her arms out, stumbling slightly – attempting to Disapparate –.)*

Damn!

(She exits. **MARTIN** *goes over to the hooded figure on the floor.)*

MARTIN. Are you ok?

GARFIELD. *(For it is he.)* Geroffme...!

MARTIN. Garfield?

*(***GARFIELD** *sits up and pulls back his hood. He is unkempt, angry and appears to be drunk.)*

GARFIELD. Go away

MARTIN. What happened?

GARFIELD. You did, you pathetic excuse for a actor

MARTIN. I'm a travel agent

GARFIELD. Then fly away little travel agent and love me in piece.

MARTIN. Thanks... why aren't you out there trying to catch Iago?

GARFIELD. I've been sacked

MARTIN. Who's running the RSC?

GARFIELD. The government cut our funding.

MARTIN. Isn't anyone doing anything about this...?

(**GARFIELD** *takes out a half drunk bottlee of green liquid, and pulls the cork out with his teeth.)*

GARFIELD. The RSC stands empty, London is overrun with villains, all the heroes have disappeared and it's all your fault. Cheers!

(**GARFIELD** *takes a swig, winces, looks at the bottle and giggles.)*

(Muttering.) Green-eyed monster... he he he – want some?

MARTIN. No thanks

GARFIELD. Suit yourself

(He takes another drink.)

MARTIN. I don't get it... you only lost your job a few months ago – why are you living like this?

(**GARFIELD** *hiccoughs and gets teary.)*

GARFIELD. My wife kicked me out!

MARTIN. She *was* sleeping with the Donkey guy –

GARFIELD. No she wasn't – why? Have you heard anything?

MARTIN. Why did she –?

(**GARFIELD** *sighs.)*

GARFIELD. We've got this boy, an orphan we adopted. I wanted him to go to drama school like me and she wanted him to go into banking... and it all got out of hand.

MARTIN. Were you really going to kill me?

GARFIELD. It was the only way I could think of making the barrier permanent… killing the last descendant – the sole person who could open or close the barrier between fiction and reality.

MARTIN. You bastard

GARFIELD. Least I didn't unleash the apocalypse.

MARTIN. You're just going to drink 'til the world ends?

GARFIELD. The heroes have gone… nothing left to do…

MARTIN. Still no idea how it's going to happen?

GARFIELD. Nope

MARTIN. Maybe…

GARFIELD. Martin, you had a chance to make a difference and you blew it. You let yourself be misled by a foolish little girl who couldn't deal with the fact she wasn't the greatest love –

*(**MARTIN** punches **GARFIELD**.)*

MARTIN. Don't you dare talk about her like that!

GARFIELD. You pushed her away!

MARTIN. Don't you think I've regretted it every moment, of every hour, of every day since then!

GARFIELD. Why aren't you looking for her?!

MARTIN. I don't know where to look!

GARFIELD. How many Juliet Capulet's do you know on Facebook?!

*(**MARTIN** goes to say something and then runs off. **GARFIELD** looks like he's about to say something, but gives up and returns to drinking. After a little moment **PUCK** emerges from the shadows. **GARFIELD** turns.)*

You...

*(**PUCK** gently taps **GARFIELD** on the head, knocking him unconscious, and then proceeds to drag him off. The lights shift.)*

(III.iii)

(Enter **IAGO**, *wearing a sharp pinstripe suit, followed by one of the* **THREE SISTERS** *making notes,* **EDMUND** *and* **LADY MACBETH** *being made up by the other two* **SISTERS** *they are putting the finishing touches to a speech.)*

IAGO. They said Shakespeare couldn't be changed. Meddling with it would only lead to disaster – would only lead to disaster...?

EDMUND. A plague on all our houses?

IAGO. Ha ha – that's good... very good... they were wrong, those... fanatical zealots jealously guarding a tradition that is outdated and out of favour –

EDMUND. The same people who thought the poor should stay poor, that no man should be elevated through his own ability but rather than by birth or kinship –

IAGO. We did not stand for it then and we will not stand for it now. We, who changed the world: the angry young men who tore through the establishment –

EDMUND. We brought you Godot and made Pinter pause. The true innovators of theatre in this country. We're going to tear up the rulebook again starting with William Shakespeare.

IAGO. We're going to rewrite history...

EDMUND. Brilliant

(One of the **SISTER** *hands the speech to* **IAGO**.*)*

IAGO. Thank you. It's done?

EDMUND. It's done

IAGO. Antonia?

LADY MACBETH. It's perfect. Well done Edmund

IAGO. Well done Edmund

LADY MACBETH. I think such good work deserves to be rewarded – what do you think dearest?

IAGO. King of England?

EDMUND. If you insist

IAGO. Done – and do you think we should –?

LADY MACBETH. I think we should –

(One of the **SISTERS** *hands a tattered copy of Othello to* **LADY MACBETH** *who gives it to* **EDMUND.***)*

IAGO. Why don't you give that a little read?

EDMUND. *Othello* – why –?

IAGO. All in good time, my villainous friend… now I have a speech to give.

*(***EDMUND** *exits with the* **THREE SISTERS. IAGO** *looks through his speech, while* **LADY MACBETH** *suddenly looks worried.)*

LADY MACBETH. Do you think he suspects?

IAGO. None of them do

LADY MACBETH. Is it going to work?

IAGO. Naturally

LADY MACBETH. I've started to hear things

*(***IAGO** *looks up.)*

IAGO. Like what?

LADY MACBETH. A few whisperings – and – I – I – can't find Dickie

IAGO. He'll turn up – he always does… no matter how many time one tries to… he'll turn up

LADY MACBETH. I know but –

*(**IAGO** turns sharply towards **LADY MACBETH.**)*

IAGO. Sister dearest – what have I told you about your guilt issues…?

*(**IAGO** gets closer to her and starts to caress her hair.)*

LADY MACBETH. It's all in my mind –

*(**IAGO** pulls **LADY MACBETH** into a hug.)*

IAGO. Everything is going to work perfectly and nobody can stop us

*(**IAGO** starts to kiss **LADY MACBETH**, which at first she resists but then surrenders to it and it is broken off by **IAGO** suddenly.)*

Excellent –

(He cups her chin and rearranges her lipstick with his thumb.)

Now chin-up – tits and teeth and –

*(He turns her round, and propels her to a side exit with a firm pat on her backside. **LADY MACBETH** stops at the doorway. We hear the sound of photographs and press.)*

LADY MACBETH. Ladies and Gentlemen – it is my great pleasure to introduce you to the next Artistic Director of the Royal Shakespeare Company: Aloysius Archibald Iago…

*(Applause as **IAGO** walks off stage to greet his public. The lights shift.)*

(III.iv)

(Lights up on **JULES** *on the other side of the stage.* **MARTIN** *enters. They stand looking at each other. An awkward pause.)*

JULES. Hello

MARTIN. Hello

JULES. I got your message

MARTIN. Good – I was – there's actually quite of lot of you on… never mind

(Pause.)

JULES. How are you?

MARTIN. Fine, you?

JULES. I miss you

MARTIN. Me too

JULES. I'm sorry

MARTIN. Me too

JULES. What you said

MARTIN. I was angry

JULES. You tore the barrier between theatre and reality –

MARTIN. I was really angry… you betrayed the RSC

JULES. I know… Mercutio died because me

MARTIN. Mercutio always dies because of you – it wasn't your fault. It was the way he was written.

JULES. I thought I wanted to change who I was, except I can't change who I am – I'll always be Juliet and I'm always going to fall in love.

MARTIN. But you did change – don't you see – you fell in love with me.

JULES. I did

*(***MARTIN*** goes up to ***JULES***.)*

MARTIN. Which means you – I think it means – I hope it means – that in some way we were always meant to be together and just because you're fictional doesn't make it any less real. I really do love you Juliet Capulet

JULES. And I love you Romeo Montague

*(***MARTIN*** looks startled.)*

Joke! – I'm joking – I love you Martin Shakespeare

*(***MARTIN*** and ***JULES*** kiss. They back off, still holding each other.)*

MARTIN. So...

JULES. So...

MARTIN. Do... you... want to... continue... anon?

JULES. What?

MARTIN. Not that we have to... I mean we could... I ...

JULES. Yes we... I mean... if you...

MARTIN. I know...

(They struggle with what to do next.)

JULES. Did you know Iago's opening his first season at the RSC with *Othello*.

MARTIN. Do we have to talk about him right now?

*(***MARTIN****'s face falls as he suddenly realises something.* ***JULES*** *doesn't notice for a while.)*

JULES. In a strange sort of way, he's responsible for bringing us together, and splitting us up – do you know I've never been dumped before. It was amazing! Moping around the flat in my pyjamas – well they weren't mine I had to borrow them off Hermia – I don't have any pyjamas – and I ate so much chocolate, drunk loads of vodka and… Martin – what's wrong?

MARTIN. I know how Iago is going to destroy the world

(The lights shift as **MARTIN** *runs off with* **JULES** *and* **EDMUND** *enters reading from Othello.)*

(III.v)

EDMUND. Soft you, a word or two before you go

I have done the state some service, and they know't

No more of that.

(Enter **LADY MACBETH**, *she is in a completely unhinged state, as per her original character.)*

LADY MACBETH. That which hath made them drunk hath made me bold. What Hath quenched them hath given me fire. Hark, peace!

EDMUND. It's only me

*(***LADY MACBETH** *stares at him strangely.)*

LADY MACBETH. It was the owl that shrieked, the fatal bellman – the fatal bellman – the – I can't find him

EDMUND. Find who?

LADY MACBETH. I've looked everywhere, but he's not there. I've searched the whole play – I can't find him... I have given suck, and know how tender 'tis to love the babe that milks me... then nothing. My baby's gone...

EDMUND. Dickie will turn up

LADY MACBETH. Who?

EDMUND. Richard III– your...

LADY MACBETH. He took him away from me

EDMUND. You mean they – the RSC

LADY MACBETH. My brother. He said it was for the best. It would make me stronger... you should have seen the look on his face, when he realised Dickie was special – he was going to kill him and had he not resembled my father as he slept, I had done't –

*(***LADY MACBETH** *screams and puts her head in his hands.* **EDMUND** *goes up to her and holds her in a tight embrace.* **LADY MACBETH** *begins to sob.)*

I don't know who I am anymore –

EDMUND. This speech of yours hath moved me,

And shall perchance do good... Antonia – who is Dickie's father?

*(***IAGO** *enters.* **LADY MACBETH** *suddenly breaks away from* **EDMUND** *and recovers her poise.)*

LADY MACBETH. It's Lady Macbeth and get your hands off me you bastard.

IAGO. You must forgive my sister – she has occasional lapses of character. Nothing to worry about

EDMUND. I ...understand

IAGO. It's a stressful time for all of – we're on the verge of an historic occasion.

EDMUND. Sure

LADY MACBETH. You're not having second thoughts, Edmund?

EDMUND. No – are you?

LADY MACBETH. Don't be ridiculous

EDMUND. But – your... Richard III?

LADY MACBETH. That monstrosity should've been put down at birth.

(An awkward silence.)

IAGO. Have you had the chance to read the script?

EDMUND. Er – *Othello*? – yes I have. I don't understand what you want me to do

IAGO. My dear boy, you're going to be the star of the show. Why don't we discuss this over dinner – there's this charming little place down the road with a chocolate soufflé you'd kill your wife to get the recipe for. You joining us, Antonia?

LADY MACBETH. I'm not hungry –

*(***IAGO** *looks intently at* **LADY MACBETH**, *unseen by* **EDMUND.***)*

Maybe a salad – you boys pop along and I'll put my face on.

IAGO. Don't be too long... my darling

*(***IAGO** *puts his arm round* **EDMUND** *and leads him off. On his exit he has a final look at* **LADY MACBETH. LADY MACBETH** *starts to rearrange her clothes and hair. As she puts her hand to her face, some mascara gets on her hand. She begins to rub her hand.)*

LADY MACBETH. Yet here's a spot!

(She walks off, still rubbing her hands.)

Out damned spot!

(III.vi)

(The lights change as **BENEDICK** *enters on his own. He walks to the front of the stage looking mournful. He looks around him furtively and…)*

BENEDICK. I have of late – but wherefore I know not – lost all my mirth, foregone all custom of exercise; and indeed it goes so heavily with my disposition this…

*(***BEATRICE** *shouts from offstage.)*

BEATRICE. *(Offstage.)* Oh no you don't!

(She marches on.)

Don't you dare!

BENEDICK. I wasn't… doing anything…

BEATRICE. I heard you!

BENEDICK. I –

BEATRICE. What did I tell you about quoting 'The Dane'! You have a perfectly decent vocabulary of your own.

BENEDICK. I know but –

BEATRICE. There's no excuse!

*(***BENEDICK** *loses all bravado and suddenly looks close to tears.)*

BENEDICK. I – I – c –

*(***BEATRICE***'s mood changes completely, and she comforts her husband.)*

BEATRICE. Darling what is it?

BENEDICK. I – I don't know who I am anymore.

BEATRICE. You're my little jester

BENEDICK. I'm serious

BEATRICE. So am I – you think it's easy for me?

BENEDICK. You're always so… in control of everything, you know what to say, you're the most beautiful woman I've ever known and even after four hundred and fourteen years I get butterflies when I see you and… I'm just a babbling idiot… I don't know what you ever saw in me.

BEATRICE. Do you remember when all they could talk about was *Romeo and Juliet* and you started pestering Shakespeare to have a suicide pact thrown into the plot.

BENEDICK. Possibly…

BEATRICE. What did he say to you?

BENEDICK. "Romeo gets the best lines but everyone will want to play you"

BEATRICE. Because you're an extraordinary, wonderful man with a heart as big as a mountain, who is cleverer, funnier and occasionally a better person than this mouthy old fool. You tamed my wild heart and I love you with so much of it. Now let me stop thy mouth.

(She goes to kiss him, just at the point of contact **BENEDICK** *speaks.)*

BENEDICK. That's my line

*(***BEATRICE** *pulls back.)*

BEATRICE. I was –

BENEDICK. *(Rushing.)* Peace let me stop thy mouth!

(He grabs and kisses her, which she responds to joyfully. **PUCK** *enters.* **BENEDICK** *notices him/her/them (delete as applicable) and drops* **BEATRICE***.)*

Traitor!

PUCK. I'm not here to fight

(**BENEDICK** *draws a sword.*)

BENEDICK. Tough

PUCK. You need to listen to what I have to say –

BEATRICE. You betrayed us – what more is there to say?

(**BENEDICK** *starts to advance on* **PUCK.**)

PUCK. It's not what you think – no – you've got it all wrong. This isn't funny anymore

BENEDICK. Of course it's not funny

PUCK. I'm not talking to you –

BENEDICK. Draw your sword

PUCK. I don't have a sword –

BENEDICK. What weapon do you have?

PUCK. I'm Puck...

(**BENEDICK** *goes up to his wife and reaches in her clothes.*)

BEATRICE. Darling, not in public...!

BENEDICK. Won't be a moment

(**BENEDICK** *takes out a dagger from* **BEATRICE***'s person and throws it towards* **PUCK.**)

Pick it up

PUCK. Don't be ridiculous

BENEDICK. I can't kill an unarmed man – woman – hobgoblin –

PUCK. Good luck!

BENEDICK. Pick it up…

PUCK. I could crush you with my –

BENEDICK. PICK IT UP!

(**PUCK** *picks up the dagger.* **BENEDICK** *advances.)*

BENEDICK. Prepare to die

*(A voice (***GARFIELD***) rings out.)*

GARFIELD. Put up your sword!

PUCK. Finally!

BENEDICK. More of your villainous friends – eh?

BEATRICE. Benedick –

BENEDICK. Not now!

BEATRICE. But it's –

(**BENEDICK** *charges,* **GARFIELD** *steps out of the shadows, back in his usual clothes and state, and disarms him.)*

– Garfield –

(**BENEDICK** *tries to recover his dignity, while arguing with his wife.)*

BENEDICK. Why didn't you say so?

BEATRICE. I did try but you were doing your whole *Gladiator* thing – I didn't want to interrupt the flow – it

BENEDICK. I looked like an idiot

BEATRICE. It was very sexy

BENEDICK. Go on…

GARFIELD. Please don't –

(**BENEDICK** *turns towards* **GARFIELD.**)

BENEDICK. Garfield – you're back – what's Puck doing with you?

GARFIELD. Puck works for me.

BEATRICE. Puck betrayed us

(*Enter* **MARTIN** *and* **JULES.**)

MARTIN. Puck's a double agent

GARFIELD. And the circle is complete –

BEATRICE. Martin! Jules!

BENEDICK. Ooh this is just like *This is Your Life*!

BEATRICE. Could you *be* any camper?

MARTIN. You wanted everyone to think they worked for the other side

GARFIELD. I did

MARTIN. To make me understand, to make us all understand –

BENEDICK. Understand what?

MARTIN. There is a force in the universe more powerful than anything known to man. It is imagination. Imagination can change people's lives in a moment and stay with them forever. We talk of science being the catalyst for the great advances of mankind, but it was imagination which made us look to the horizon and wonder what was beyond it. Imagination makes anything possible and harnessing it is one of the true skills one can achieve in theatre. The most skilled of all was a remarkable man called William Shakespeare – whose imagination was such that his characters quite literally came to life. But this kind of power has to be controlled, there must be rules. That's why the rules of theatre are so important. And that's why when these rules fall into the hands a four hundred year old supervillain, whose only motivation is to destroy everything good in the world, then we should be truly afraid. Iago is going to break the rules of theatre by rewriting *Othello*. Becoming Artistic Director of the RSC gave him access to the original version of every single play Shakespeare wrote. The rules have just enough flexibility to allow lines to be cut or the occasional character to be excised but he is going further. He's planning to change the plot, and with it the fundamental structure of theatre will crumble, and chaos will reign. Very soon entire genres will be mixed: in the beginning it will seem a brilliantly novel idea until the idea becomes more important than the subject itself. Comedy becomes tragedy, monologues become one-liners and fast paced dialogue morph into epic diatribes on the state of the world. Characters are confused and motivation is lost. A bedroom farce is turned in the blink of an eye to a sado-masochistic exploration of sexual deviancy in married couples; Greek tragedies become vaudevillian romps with the Chorus replaced by a chorus line; kitchen-sink dramas into bare stage Performance Art where relationships are represented by a tree and a bucket and even Godot will turn up five minutes into the play and they'll all be in the pub singing "*Danny Boy*". Imagination will turn in on itself, and bring only despair. It will unleash a volcano of destruction into reality, enveloping the world in corrupted lava of confusion. This toxic cloud of incomprehensible artistic influence will choke the life out of rational thought. The natural evolution of change will speed up to catastrophic proportions. The desperate desire to come up with the next big idea will become more and more dangerous. Fifteen minutes of fame reduced to fifteen seconds. Reality TV resorting to programmes like Celebrity Execution just to keep up with the trend. School syllabuses will grow and grow. Lessons reduced in length to allow more subjects to be taught in a day. The information overload will intensify to such an extent that concepts men and women have spent their entire lives studying, will be boiled down to meaningless sentences, phrases, single words and eventually just sounds. These sounds will grow until individual meaning is drowned out and all that is left is a chorus of noise which builds to a deafening roar, raging like a torrent around the world until voices are torn to shreds, the roar reduced to a whisper and then nothing. And in this final moment of absolute stillness will come the horrific realisation: there are no more ideas left. Imagination has been completely extinguished and life has no purpose anymore. The silent mass of humanity will share a brief moment of silent despair before surrendering themselves completely, shutting down to the most basic functions until even they seem pointless and shortly after every single human being on the planet will just… stop.

(A silence.)

BENEDICK. Blimey…

GARFIELD. Indeed

BENEDICK. I thought Garfield went on – but that's got to be a record

(**GARFIELD** *nods to* **PUCK**, *who heads to the side of the stage and gestures off.)*

PUCK. It's alright, don't be frightened…

(**RICHARD III** *shuffles on. He stands looking at everyone.)*

GARFIELD. We found him in a car park in Leicester.

(**RICHARD III** *adopts his opening stance, opens his mouth and hesitates. He tries again but nothing comes out. He begins to panic.*

He slowly begins to stand up straight, his hunch disappearing. General shock.)

MARTIN. They're losing their identity.

GARFIELD. They don't belong here –

MARTIN. That's why Shakespeare created the barrier – the line between fiction and reality should never have been crossed and I have to put it back.

GARFIELD. This time it has to be for good –

(**JULES** *steps forward.)*

JULES. He can't die

GARFIELD. He doesn't need to die to recreate the barrier but –

PUCK. The barrier wasn't just for his villains.

BEATRICE. Oh no

(A sudden realisation.)

GARFIELD. The only reason the gaps in the barrier were created was so fictional characters could help the RSC in the struggle against Iago – but now we know that's too much of a risk. We have to make it –

JULES. Permanent

MARTIN. It's OK – you can stay with me

GARFIELD. Without a character there is no play.

MARTIN. Then I can stay in the theatre world

GARFIELD. You're not fictional…

(Pause as it sinks in.)

I'm so sorry

MARTIN. I can't – it's too much – I can't choose –

JULES. Martin, you are the last living descendant of William Shakespeare and it is your duty to protect your world... no matter what the cost.

MARTIN. I can't lose you. I've only just found you... again.

JULES. Please – don't make this harder than it is

MARTIN. You're right – you're absolutely right – I quit

(General shock.)

GARFIELD. What?

JULES. But the end of the world?

MARTIN. If I lose you it will be the end of the world

(Silence.)

Come with me

JULES. I – I – please don't make me do this

GARFIELD. You're our only hope

MARTIN. No I'm not! I can't be – I'm no one – OK so I somehow know all of Shakespeare's work off by heart – but I'm nobody. I'm just a travel agent from Stratford who's in way over his head, and I'm going to do what I always do in this situation and walk away. Jules... I'm not expecting you to come with me now, but I'll wait for you.

*(**MARTIN** leaves.)*

BENEDICK. That was unexpected

GARFIELD. He is our only hope

BEATRICE. He'll come round

GARFIELD. What if he doesn't?

JULES. He won't have a choice

*(Everyone turns to **JULES**.)*

When it happens – when the barrier is back up – will I – remember him?

GARFIELD. No

JULES. Martin?

GARFIELD. Leave that to me

*(***JULES*** nods and takes out her mobile, dialling a number, as she goes.)*

JULES. Hello – Friar Laurence – it's Jules – I need you to do me a favour

GARFIELD. Whatever happens the performance of *Othello* must be completed as it was originally written. We may have no heroes to help us and the Last Descendant has run away but there's a happy few of us who might just be able to make a stand – so... whose up for storming the RSC and saving the world...!

(General cheer. Everyone leaves, with **PUCK** *and* **RICHARD III** *last,* **PUCK** *tries to coax Richard to go with her but Richard suddenly runs away from him and in the direction* **MARTIN** *left. The lights change.)*

ACT FOUR

(IV.i)

(Enter **TYBALT** *with a briefcase handcuffed to his wrist. Enter* **IAGO**, *who goes up to the briefcase, checks something and turns towards the front of the stage, and chuckles to himself.)*

IAGO. Do you know Tybalt – in the course of all this excitement – I haven't had the chance to deliver a really good soliloquy. So, in this calm before the storm, I thought I'd take the opportunity, as the villain of the piece, to give a little soupçon of my devious plan. As you see there is no hero tied up to expound this diatribe to, so that they might effect an impossible escape and save the world – it doesn't work like that. Sometimes the villains win. And I am going to win. The Last Descendant does give one pause for thought, and by now he should have worked out the full extent of my ambition. I have plans for him of course – victory is assured – oh happy day – calloo callay. Now, Garfield Oberon was almost a decent adversary, but like his predecessors he always underestimated my bottomless pit of evil. It is pure unadulterated malevolence that flows through my veins. I haven't an ounce of conscience in my body. I have Shakespeare to thank for that. Why then, do I insist on destroying his legacy and with it the entire world? Because I can. Because I only know what it is to destroy and never feel remorse. I turned a man of integrity and honour into a gibbering psychotic wreck and I thought to myself "why stop there?" I was created a villain. I –

(**EDMUND** *has entered and is hovering.)*

Can't you see I'm in the middle of a self-aggrandizing speech?!

EDMUND. I – I'm sorry to bother you. It's just – well – things aren't quite – this isn't what I signed up for

IAGO. Are you having second thoughts?

EDMUND. I have my – doubts

IAGO. My dear boy, of course you do. It's how you were written. Your character repents at the end of *King Lear* doesn't he?

EDMUND. Yes

IAGO. Everyone always bloody repents – even Othello. I turn him into the greatest villain since, well, me and what does he do to repay me? He goes and kills himself. It's all the same: death or repentance. Do you know the only character who doesn't recant of his crimes in Shakespeare is me? I'm the only remorseless son of a bitch in all thirty six of his plays and I'm sick of it! So tonight we're going to change all that. Tonight we are performing the original version of *Othello*, as written by William Shakespeare – until we reach the final scene when the Moor – will be suddenly saved from his suicidal end by the timely intervention of one Edmund, Bastard Son of Gloucester, lately arrived from England with his army where he did not perish as was previously thought at the end of King Lear, disarms Othello and forces him to face the justice of his crime, while at the same time providing a cast iron alibi for me. Othello's nobility of spirit will allow him to face trial for the murder, not before he promotes me to general and then with our two armies we shall begin our conquest.

EDMUND. You're going to invade the rest of Shakespeare's work?

IAGO. The ones set in Italy and France shouldn't put up too much of a fight. We'll bastardise the bard!

EDMUND. I don't want to be part of this anymore...

IAGO. Really?

EDMUND. It's madness!

*(***IAGO*** goes to* **TYBALT** *who hold out the briefcase.* **IAGO** *takes out a key, opens the briefcase and takes out a script.)*

IAGO. This is the original script of *King Lear*

EDMUND. You wouldn't –

IAGO. I can't decide between writing you out of existence or redrafting you as a high pitched eunuch with body odour issues.

EDMUND. Can I make another suggestion?

IAGO. By all means

EDMUND. Let's do everything you want.

IAGO. Good idea.

*(***IAGO*** hands the script back to* **TYBALT** *without looking.* **EDMUND** *turns to leave. He hesitates.)*

EDMUND. Um –

IAGO. Yes?!

EDMUND. Did you know your sister's completely lost her mind?

IAGO. Not again – Sister!

(Enter **FIRST SISTER.***)*

FIRST SISTER. Yes master?

IAGO. Bring her to me

FIRST SISTER. Yes master

(**FIRST SISTER** *exits.* **IAGO** *walks up to* **EDMUND** *and stands very close to him.)*

IAGO. Consider yourself lucky you have lines to speak tonight. Someone else once chose to defy me, so I ripped out his vocal cords. Isn't that right Tybalt?

(**TYBALT** *looks pained.* **FIRST SISTER** *reenters with* **LADY MACBETH.** *She is in a dishevelled state –.)*

LADY MACBETH. Fie my lord! Fie! A soldier and afeard? What need we fear who knows it, when none can call our power to accompt? Yet who would have thought the old man to have so much blood in him?

IAGO. Hold her down

EDMUND. What?

LADY MACBETH. The Thane of Fife had a wife: where is she now?

(**IAGO** *goes to* **TYBALT** *who hands him a vial.)*

IAGO. She's reverting to her script form. This'll suppress it. Hold her down!

(**FIRST SISTER** *and* **EDMUND** *hold her down)*

LADY MACBETH. Here's the smell of the blood still: all the perfumes of Arabia will not sweeten this little hand.

(**IAGO** *forces the vial contents down her throat. He then moves back to* **TYBALT** *who hands him a towel and he returns the empty vial – a well practised routine.* **LADY MACBETH** *screams.)*

Oh! Oh! Oh!

IAGO. Shouldn't be too long –

(**LADY MACBETH** *begins to calm.*)

LADY MACBETH. *(Weakly.)* What's done cannot be undone –

IAGO. Take her away

(**FIRST SISTER** *leads* **LADY MACBETH** *off. Just as she exits,* **FIRST SISTER** *glances back at* **IAGO.**)

Tybalt – kill Martin Shakespeare

(**TYBALT** *bows and leaves.*)

Oh and Edmund –

(**EDMUND** *looks expectantly.*)

Release the villains.

(**EDMUND** *leaves.* **IAGO** *exits in a different direction, still reading the parchment. The lights change.*)

(IV.ii)

(Enter MARTIN. *He is talking on his mobile. As the conversation continues,* TYBALT *enters noiselessly from behind and approaches* MARTIN. *As he draws closer he takes out a dagger and prepares to stab him in the back.)*

MARTIN. No Mum – I just think that maybe you're overreacting – well it's not like I can – what was I supposed to do – that's not the point – what do you mean I'll get over her like the last ones – she's – she's not that much older than me – well... no I ...no Mum... well maybe stocking up on tinned food and bottled water might be a good idea but –

*(*TYBALT *is about to plunge the knife in when* RICHARD III *runs screaming towards them both and barrels into* TYBALT *who is knocked to the floor, seemingly unconscious.)*

*(*RICHARD III *turns towards* MARTIN *and smiles. He goes to walk forward, but somehow can't. He reaches down, feels his stomach and then shows* MARTIN *a hand that it's covered in blood. He collapses.)*

No!

(Before MARTIN *has a chance to react* TYBALT *leaps to his feet, still holding the dagger and advances towards* MARTIN *at speed.* TYBALT *pulls back his dagger and at the last moment* MARTIN *neatly sidesteps* TYBALT. TYBALT *turns again and heads back to* MARTIN *and tries to stab him again, which* MARTIN *blocks without completely being aware of what he's doing.* TYBALT *tries this a number of times, each time* MARTIN *growing in confidence.*

Finally **MARTIN** *disarms* **TYBALT** *and punches him in the face.* **TYBALT** *runs off.* **MARTIN** *goes up to* **RICHARD III.**)

You saved my life

RICHARD III. Advance our standards, Set upon our foes!

Our ancient word of courage, fair Saint George

Inspire us with the spleen of fiery dragons.

Upon them! Victory sits on our helms!

(**RICHARD III** *dies.* **PUCK** *enters.*)

PUCK. Leave him to me, you have more important things to do

(**MARTIN** *stands.*)

MARTIN. What do I do?

PUCK. Bring back the heroes

(*Faint music as* **MARTIN** *leaves, and* **PUCK** *takes* **RICHARD III** *offstage. The lights change.*)

(IV.iii)

(There is a loud explosion. Enter **BENEDICK, BEATRICE** *and* **GARFIELD**. *They are all carrying swords and covered in dust.)*

BENEDICK. I'm going to kill Prospero – I just had this dry-cleaned

GARFIELD. We needed a diversion

BEATRICE. It was a bit excessive

BENEDICK. Is it just me, or does the place seem strangely deserted?

BEATRICE. Maybe you got the wrong theatre

BENEDICK. Are you questioning my sense of direction?

(As the argument continues. The stage begins to slowly darken, which goes unnoticed for a little while.)

BEATRICE. You could have stopped and asked

BENEDICK. I knew where I was going

BEATRICE. Like the time we were going to Hero's house

BENEDICK. It was a shortcut

BEATRICE. We ended up in Venice

(A low rumbling (of voices) begins, it grows steadily louder. **GARFIELD** *notices this and the stage darkening, and shadows appear at the periphery of the stage.)*

BENEDICK. You read the map wrong

BEATRICE. I read the –! You were navigating by the stars –

BENEDICK. As men of old did

GARFIELD. Guys –

BEATRICE. You thought the North Star was the Moon

BENEDICK. You never sought to correct me –

BEATRICE. I did – I said –

*(**BEATRICE** notices the phenomena as well. **BENEDICK** does not.)*

BENEDICK. No! No! You just sat there in stony silence, with that look on your face you usually reserve for the bedroom when I want to have se –

BEATRICE. Benedick

BENEDICK. That's the voice you use –

BEATRICE. Benedick!

BENEDICK. Benedick! Benedick! It really gets on my ti –

*(**BEATRICE** silences him by grabbing his head and pointing him in the direction the noise is coming from.)*

What the fu –?

(The noise grows louder. There are shadows and the voices of numerous Shakespeare Villains emerge from everywhere, giving the sense of a mass army.)

GARFIELD. Shakespeare's Villains

BENEDICK. My god...

BEATRICE. We're completely outnumbered

GARFIELD. We can't surrender

BEATRICE. We can't fight them all – there are whole armies out there

GARFIELD. I'll try and talk to them

BENEDICK. Negotiation – good idea

(**GARFIELD** *steps forward.*)

GARFIELD. What do I say?

BEATRICE. Please don't kill us...?

GARFIELD. My name is Garfield Oberon, I am the true Artistic Director of the Royal Shakespeare Company. I command you to leave us in peace.

(The lights flicker even more and Villains grow louder.)

It didn't work

BEATRICE. Try talking in our language

GARFIELD. Two households! Both alike in dignity...

(The voices build.)

BENEDICK. O for a muse of fire...

(The voices build.)

BEATRICE. If music be the food of love –

(The voices continue to build.)

GARFIELD. It's not working

BENEDICK. I'm too young to die!

BEATRICE. You're four hundred and fifteen!

(Seemingly out of nowhere, heroic music starts and builds. **[MUSIC: GUSTAV MAHLER'S MOVEMENT V. IM TEMPO DES SHERZO"]*** *There are muffled blasts of white light shooting across the stage as the*

---

* A licence to produce THE SHAKESPEARE CONSPIRACY and use GUSTAV MAHLER'S [MOVEMENT V. IM TEMPO DES SHERZO] does not include a performance licence for any third-party or copyrighted recordings. Licensees should create their own.

doors open. Out of the first door walks one of Shakespeare's Heroes with their sword drawn. Their face is obscured by a helmet, but a large skull emblazoned on his chest gives away that he is Hamlet. In time with the music a second helmeted hero enters from another door, with a large "V" emblazoned on their chest (Henry V), while out of Hamlet's door walks another hero with a heart on their chest (Romeo). Finally **MARTIN** *emerges last, wearing attire suiting someone who is on a mission to save the world – a cross between the emblems of Shakespeare's English Kings and a superhero. He walks to the front and draws his sword, which is matched by the others heroes.)*

MARTIN. Once more unto the breach dear friends – Cry God for Harry, England and Saint George!

(We hear a battle roar, as **MARTIN** *and the heroes charge off stage. Music fades as the sounds of a fight begins.)*

GARFIELD. Follow them! Whatever happens – *Othello* has to be finished as it was written.

BEATRICE. What about you?

GARFIELD. I'm going to get my old job back.

*(***BENEDICK** *and* **BEATRICE** *draw their swords and exit.* **GARFIELD** *exits in a different direction. The lights change.)*

(IV.iv)

(The battle sounds increase. **[MUSIC: GUSTAV MAHLER'S "MOVEMENT V. IM TEMPO DES SHERZO"]***. *We hear swords clashing, the sounds of armies charging each other, cannon fire, possibly a couple of lightsabres and TIE fighters.)*

(One of the Heroes comes on fighting a Villain (ideally an identifiable but masked character).)

*(***EDMUND** *leaps on stage, fighting* **BENEDICK. BEATRICE** *follows trying to get involved – at one point she goes to jump in but* **BENEDICK** *holds her back.)*

BENEDICK. Not now darling!

(In the next moment **EDMUND** *gets* **BENEDICK** *in a precarious position, and is about to finish him off when.)*

Now darling!

*(***BEATRICE** *blocks* **EDMUND***'s blow, which he easily counters by disarming her and sending her sword flying to the back,* **BENEDICK** *and* **EDMUND** *continue their fight, while* **BEATRICE** *goes to retrieve her sword.* **LADY MACBETH** *enters armed, sees* **BEATRICE** *bending down and runs towards her with a scream.* **BEATRICE** *turns helpless. Out of*

---

* A licence to produce THE SHAKESPEARE CONSPIRACY and use GUSTAV MAHLER'S [MOVEMENT V. IM TEMPO DES SHERZO] does not include a performance licence for any third-party or copyrighted recordings. Licensees should create their own.

nowhere the **THIRD SISTER** *appears, whips out her wand out and yells.)*

THIRD SISTER. EXPELLIARMUS!!!!

(Whether by surprise or magic – we shall never know – **LADY MACBETH** *drops her sword. The* **THIRD SISTER** *punches the air with joy and disappears.* **BEATRICE** *has enough time to grab her weapon, and the two ladies rise and fight each other. The two fights become one.)*

*(***TYBALT** *hurtles in being utterly taken to the cleaners by* **MARTIN**, *who is fighting like a man possessed. It's so intense that the other fighters briefly pause to watch. As they head off the other side of the stage,* **MARTIN** *can be heard shouting.)*

MARTIN. My name is Martin Shakespeare, you killed my brother – prepare to die!

(Both **LADY MACBETH** *and* **EDMUND** *use the distraction to make a run for it, in either direction. Just before they run off,* **BENEDICK** *grabs* **BEATRICE** *for a quick kiss.)*

BENEDICK. I love you!

BEATRICE. I know.

(They run off chasing their respective enemies. **IAGO** *walks on carrying the briefcase, which he lays down on a table. Enter* **GARFIELD.***)*

GARFIELD. Good evening, Iago

IAGO. Good evening Garfield, so kind of you to drop in

GARFIELD. I wouldn't have missed it for the world –

IAGO. I almost considered you a decent adversary but –

GARFIELD. Oh kill me now!

IAGO. It can be arranged –

GARFIELD. If I have to listen another rambling soliloquy of yours… I didn't come here for this –

IAGO. What did you come here for?

GARFIELD. Aloysius Archibald Iago, by the authority vested in me by the Royal Shakespeare Company I arrest you for crimes against theatre.

IAGO. You fool! I *am* the Royal Shakespeare Company.

GARFIELD. Then in accordance with the statutes of old, I formally challenge you for the Artistic Directorship.

IAGO. Interview with the board or act off?

(**GARFIELD** *holds his sword up.)*

The old fashioned way… oh goody

*(***IAGO** *walks the back, taking off his jacket, and kicks a filing cabinet, there's a metallic clunking, and he draws out a sword from the cabinet with his left hand. There is a quick preparation, they salute each other, a first skirmish – nobody wins.* **GARFIELD** *then takes off his jacket to reveal to reveal a muscular frame.* **IAGO** *takes off his shirt to reveal a tailor made pin stripe vest, matching his suit.)*

(A second skirmish. **IAGO** *gets the upper hand and sends* **GARFIELD** *into a corner.* **GARFIELD** *laughs, turns slowly and pulls off his eye patch – revealing a perfectly good eye and advances to the centre of the stage, and does a Morpheus style come and get me. A half beat later* **IAGO** *throws the sword from his left hand to his right, does an elaborate twirl*

showing it's his better hand, while **GARFIELD***'s face falls and they begin the main body of the fight, as athletically and awesomely as possible.)*

(The final moment of the fight ends with **IAGO** *blocking a blow to his head without seeing it, revealing he is a considerably better fighter than* **GARFIELD***, brutally disarming* **GARFIELD***, cutting him several times and sending him flying into the side wall of the stage.)*

(Snarling.) What did you expect – you pathetic excuse for a director? Did you think you could take me on? Did you think all that stage combat training at the RSC was really going to help?!! What special move did you think you could come up with – little human insect?!!! What could you possibly have to conquer an undefeatable soldier steeped in four hundred years of close combat fighting and military tactics...? What do you have?!!

(Half beat.)

GARFIELD. We have a Puck

(A rumbling of thunder as **IAGO***'s sword goes flying out of his hand, as if moved by an invisible force. He suddenly doubles over in pain as if punched hard. He screams and throws a wild punch, which goes into slow motion as* **PUCK** *runs in real time across the stage punching* **IAGO** *in the face, as soon as* **PUCK** *disappears out of view, time speeds up again, as* **IAGO** *cries out in pain and looks wildly about him.)*

IAGO. Where are you?!

*(***PUCK** *leaps onto a table and (where the staging is possible), leaps off it with arms outstretched towards* **IAGO***.)*

PUCK. PUCK SMASH!!!

*(***PUCK** *crashes her arms down on* **IAGO***'s head, who is instantly crushed to the floor (again subject to staging) and left senseless.)*

*(***PUCK** *goes up to* **GARFIELD** *and helps him up.)*

GARFIELD. Thanks sweet Puck

PUCK. You're welcome

(We hear a woman's scream offstage. **BEATRICE** *runs on.)*

BEATRICE. The queen my Lord, is dead.

(A moment later, **MARTIN** *runs on fighting both* **EDMUND** *and* **TYBALT**. **EDMUND** *gets intercepted by* **BEATRICE***.)*

What have you done with my husband?!

*(***EDMUND** *laughs wickedly.* **BEATRICE** *shrieks with rage and charges him,* **EDMUND** *panics and runs off. The* **THREE SISTERS** *enter, and time slows down to reveal* **JULES** *back in her outfit at the start, in the middle of them, taking a drink from a bottle, before the* **THREE SISTERS** *disperse leaving* **JULES** *in the middle of the stage, astonishing everyone.* **TYBALT** *reacts quickest, and runs towards* **JULES**, *grabbing her and dragging her offstage at sword point. Before they completely leave,* **JULES** *manages to throw the bottle towards* **GARFIELD***.)*

MARTIN. Jules no!

*(**MARTIN** charges off in their direction. **GARFIELD** and **PUCK** run towards the door but there is a massive explosion which propels **GARFIELD** backwards – **PUCK** is not affected. Dust and detritus pour in from the side. **GARFIELD** tries to get to his feet, while at the same time out of the side of the stage stumbles **BENEDICK** and **BEATRICE**, covered in dust and scratches, coughing and spluttering but supporting each other.*

BENEDICK. The Globe's on fire!

GARFIELD. What happened?

BENEDICK. Your namesake tried to end it all with one spell which apparently was the same idea all the other supernatural characters had and the whole place went off –

GARFIELD. What about the play, did they manage to finish *Othello*?

BEATRICE. We don't know – it's carnage out there.

GARFIELD. Go and see what...

*(Before anyone can move **MARTIN** walks on carrying the body of **JULES**.)*

BEATRICE. No!

*(**MARTIN** lays her body down.)*

GARFIELD. Is she –?

*(**MARTIN** looks up at him and doesn't need to say anything, he returns his attention to **JULES**. In the chaos, nobody has noticed **IAGO** come round, and begin to move across the stage. When everyone's attention is turned*

to **JULES**, *he runs to the briefcase and takes a piece of parchment, with a cry of triumph.)*

Iago – no!

IAGO. How can you finish a play if the end doesn't exist –?

*(***IAGO** *eats the final page of Othello.)*

GARFIELD. What did you do?!

IAGO. Call it my insurance policy!

GARFIELD. At least this way I get to kill you –

*(***GARFIELD** *advances on* **IAGO** *with his sword raised.* **MARTIN** *looks up suddenly.)*

MARTIN. No...

(The lights shift, everyone freezes except **MARTIN** *as the* **THREE SISTERS** *return to the stage. Music.**)

FIRST SISTER. Then do the state some service, smite him thus

SECOND SISTER. To be or not to be it must be braved

THIRD SISTER. With end it starts again, ere world is saved

MARTIN. It was you – you made the prophecy.

(They nod sombrely.)

Do you have it?

(They smile. **SECOND SISTER** *takes out a dagger and hands it to* **MARTIN**, *who*

---

* A licence to produce THE SHAKESPEARE CONSPIRACY does not include a performance licence for any third-party or copyrighted music. Licensees should create an original composition or use music in the public domain. For further information, please see Music Use Note on page iii.

considers it as they disappear as the lights shift and time returns to normal once more.)

...wait!

*(**GARFIELD** stops. **MARTIN** stands and goes up to **IAGO**.)*

Congratulations

IAGO. Thank you

MARTIN. The only person who made my life worth living is gone.

IAGO. I wasn't anything to with that

MARTIN. I know – but it makes what I have to do a lot easier.

*(**MARTIN** stabs **IAGO**. After crying out in pain. **IAGO** laughs contemptuously.)*

IAGO. I bleed sir, but am not killed

MARTIN. Exactly...

*(**IAGO**'s face falls as he starts to realize.)*

IAGO. No –

MARTIN. You didn't destroy the original copy of the play. That flows in my veins. It is the legacy of my ancestor, William Shakespeare, and I know just what he'd want me to say.

*(**MARTIN** walks to the centre of the stage. Music.)*

Soft you, a word or two before you go

I have done the state some service, and they know't

No more of that. I pray you, in your letters,

When you shall these unlucky deeds relate,

Speak of me as I am. Nothing extenuate,
Nor set down aught in malice. Then you must speak
Of one that loved not wisely but too well,
Of one not easily jealous, but being wrought
Perplexed in the extreme; of one whose hand
Like the base Indian, threw a pearl away
Richer than all his tribe; of one whose subdued eyes
Albeit unused to the melting mood,
Drop tears as fast as the Arabian trees
Their medicinable gum. Set you down this
And say besides that in Aleppo once,
Where a malignant and a turbaned Turk
Beat a Venetian and traduced the state
I took by th' throat the circumcised dog
And smote him thus.

*(*MARTIN *stabs himself, collapsing to the floor. He drags himself towards* JULES.*)*

I killed thee ere I killed thee. No way but this
Killing myself, to die upon a kiss

(He kisses JULES *and dies… the music fades. There is a stunned silence interrupted by choked laughter and applause from* IAGO, *who walks up to* MARTIN *with his back to the audience.)*

IAGO. Bravo! Marvellous death – if the Academy gave an award for most pointless demise – Martin would win by a mile! Did no one point out that if he's dead – he can't write the end of the play… *(Mocking.)* the Last

Descendant will save us... he holds the key to our salvation... you fools! You've all been deluding your –

(**IAGO** *turns towards the front of the stage and looks shocked.*)

– self

(Pause.)

PUCK. Something wrong, Iago?

(**IAGO** *points at the audience, who have suddenly become visible.*)

IAGO. What are all those *people* doing there?

PUCK. They're watching you

IAGO. Who are they?

PUCK. The audience

IAGO. Impossible

PUCK. You're fictional again

IAGO. No... no...

(**IAGO** *suddenly doubles up in agony.*)

GARFIELD. Take him away.

(**BEATRICE** *and* **BENEDICK** *grab* **IAGO**. *He breaks free and runs to the front of the stage, He suddenly looks terrified and incredibly sad as he appeals to the audience.*)

IAGO. Please... I'm begging you... don't make me go back there. Don't make me become him. You don't understand what's it's like... I don't want to be...

(**IAGO** *doubles over again.* **BENEDICK** *and* **BEATRICE** *get hold of him again.* **IAGO** *snaps his body up straight and suddenly becomes* *a very different* **IAGO** *– the one written by William Shakespeare.)*

Demand me nothing. What you know, you know

From this time forth I will never speak to you.

*(***IAGO** *comes back to life and is dragged off screaming by* **BENEDICK** *and* **BEATRICE**, *leaving* **GARFIELD** *and* **PUCK** *standing over* **MARTIN** *and* **JULES**. *The lights change.)*

ACT FIVE

(V.i)

GARFIELD. Is that it – we win but the heroes die? There's something we're not seeing here – something I've missed –

PUCK. Why did Jules throw that bottle at you?

GARFIELD. The bottle – of course – Friar Laurence –

PUCK. It was the way she was written

BOTH. Oh no...

*(**JULES** sits bolt upright, gasping for air.)*

GARFIELD. Jules

JULES. Did it work?

*(**GARFIELD** and **PUCK** are lost for words. **JULES** looks down and sees **MARTIN**. After a while she reaches out and brushes his hair with his hand, leans down and kisses him.)*

Thy lips are warm

*(She picks up his dagger, **GARFIELD** rushes over and take the dagger off her.)*

GARFIELD. No – no – no – not you as well.

JULES. What are you doing?

GARFIELD. We thought you were... it's the way you were written.

JULES. No – it's the way Juliet was written. I'm Jules.

GARFIELD. I don't understand.

JULES. Martin closed the barrier so no one could get back into reality.

PUCK. Of course – he closed it while he was on the theatre side – thus reforming the permanent divide between theatre and reality...

JULES. And because he was on this side everything that had happened was made fictional. Everything including... Martin himself

(Pause.)

GARFIELD. So I'm... fictional...?

PUCK. Yes and no – I've become a fictional version of the Puck who Martin encountered when Mercutio died, in the same way Jules doesn't have to kill herself like Juliet, because this is a completely different story.

GARFIELD. It is?

JULES. Yes!

GARFIELD. I'm beginning to understand why Martin was so confused at the beginning. What about the "real" world?

PUCK. In the real world it will seem as if someone just made all this up and put it in a play. The RSC will just be a theatre company and Shakespeare a very good writer, who everyone hated at school but came to love as they got older. Most importantly all his characters are back where they should be: immortalised on the page.

(Pause.)

GARFIELD. I suppose when you think about it, the whole story seems too unbelievable to be real – the RSC is a branch of the government...

PUCK. The last living descendant of William Shakespeare saving the world...

Iago and Lady Macbeth as brother and sister...

GARFIELD. Romeo being gay!

*(**GARFIELD** laughs, **PUCK** doesn't. Pause.)*

Martin's still dead

JULES. No he isn't!

PUCK. What's the main difference between a real person and a fictional one?

GARFIELD. *(Getting it.)* A real person can die, whereas a fictional person lives forever within the confines of their own story... and as long as people keep reading, performing or watching them and even if they die at the end of their tale...

PUCK. You can return to the beginning.

GARFIELD. *With end it starts again...* now if we are going to make this work we need to remember exactly how this all began – you and I were standing in the shadows and – Part One: Act One – Darkness...

*(The lights begin to shift, as **GARFIELD** describes the stage directions, to the state it was at the beginning of the play (with the real world and the theatre world.)*

The stage is divided into two areas: the "real" world and the "theatre" world. Music

*(Music plays**. **GARFIELD** *and* **PUCK** *are now in the position they were in at the start of the play, in shadow.)*

Lights up on a young man – Martin...!

(The lights slowly increases on **MARTIN**, *the music builds but nothing seems to happen.* **GARFIELD** *looks around him desperately.)*

Come on! Please! Lights up on a young man – MARTIN!!

(After a moment, the music and lights swell and **MARTIN** *slowly rises and comes back to life.)*

PUCK. It worked!

*(***MARTIN** *smiles at* **JULES**, *who jumps on him and they embrace passionately. The music fades (but not completely).)*

GARFIELD. If you two could hurry up.

(One last kiss.)

You'll see each other soon – in fact you'll be together for eternity – now please get to your positions so we can finish this –

PUCK. You mean start this –

GARFIELD. Shut up –

*(***JULES** *exits and* **MARTIN** *walks towards his first position. He looks down and turns*

---

* A licence to produce THE SHAKESPEARE CONSPIRACY does not include a performance licence for any third-party or copyrighted music. Licensees should create an original composition or use music in the public domain. For further information, please see Music Use Note on page iii.

back to **GARFIELD** *and* **PUCK** *pointing at his costume. As if on cue the* **THREE SISTERS** *emerge with the costumes that* **MARTIN, GARFIELD** *and* **PUCK** *were all wearing at the start of the play, and quickly help with putting them on.)*

PUCK. What are we going to call it?

GARFIELD. The... *Shakespeare Conspiracy*?

PUCK. Right...

GARFIELD. It's just a working title

PUCK. You're the boss

GARFIELD. One thing's going to really mess with my head –

PUCK. What's that?

GARFIELD. Have I always been fictional?

(They take a small moment to think about it for a bit.)

PUCK. Yep – that one's gonna fester

(Everyone is now ready.)

GARFIELD. Now where was I – oh yes: Lights up on a young man... Martin

(Lights up on **MARTIN** *as he was for the beginning of the play.* **GARFIELD** *takes* **PUCK***'s hat out of his pocket and gives it to him,* **PUCK** *puts it on. Music starts**. **MARTIN** *looks towards the real world and inclines his head in gratitude.* **GARFIELD** *returns the gesture.)*

---

*A licence to produce THE SHAKESPEARE CONSPIRACY does not include a performance licence for any third-party or copyrighted music. Licensees should create an original composition or use music in the public domain. For further information, please see Music Use Note on page iii.

PUCK. Sir – that was genius

GARFIELD. No, Robin, Shakespeare was a genius. We just work for his Theatre Company.

(**GARFIELD** *puts his hat on.* **MUSIC: GUSTAV MAHLER'S ["MOVEMENT V. IM TEMPO DES SHERZO"]*** *Music builds to a crescendo and the music can play the rest of the play out if timed right, climax and the play begins again…)*

THE END… OR BEGINNING… DEPENDING ON HOW YOU LOOK AT IT

*A licence to produce THE SHAKESPEARE CONSPIRACY and use GUSTAV MAHLER'S [MOVEMENT V. IM TEMPO DES SHERZO] does not include a performance licence for any third-party or copyrighted recordings. Licensees should create their own.

A NOTE ON MUSIC

Given the epic nature of the play I would highly recommend looking at punctuating the play with epic music, particularly in the second half when the play becomes a full blown superhero movie on stage. Our composer of choice was Gustav Mahler – a well documented influence on John Williams – and we used Symphony Number 2: Resurrection, Movement V as our framework. PRS notwithstanding, there are a selection of moments which we found in the symphony that took the play to another level. If you do want to go another way, I'd highly recommend giving these a listen to get in the mood in rehearsal.

Mahler Symphony Number 2: Ressurrection, Movement V. D. Although the music itself is in the public domain, licensees should ensure that, if they use a recording, they secure the appropriate licences to do so – or record their own. Please see Music Use Note.

ABOUT THE AUTHOR

Andrew Shepherd put his law degree to good use by training at LAMDA as an actor. His first full length play, *Therapy*, was part of Newcastle University's takeover of Northern Stage's Guilbenkian Studio in 2000, and his Edinburgh Fringe debut, *Whispers in the Wood*, transferred to New York (St Mark's Theater) in 2002. His other work includes *The Trial of Sir Henry Irving (Lately Deceased)*, later reworked as *The Knight from Nowhere* (Park Theatre) and 20 short pieces for schoolchildren originally written for a school in Singapore. He is the Artistic Director of ACSRandom and is currently Executive Director of Theatre503, the country's leading venue for early career playwrights. His love of Shakespeare was sparked prior to his first visit to Stratford when his father handed him a copy of the Complete Works and solidified when he played Puck on stage at school. He has directed a number of his works (determined to stage them all if time allows), his wedding reception was at Shakespeare's Globe and his daughter is named Ophelia Beatrice in honour of two notable performances by his wife.

Lightning Source UK Ltd.
Milton Keynes UK
UKHW020939120622
404255UK00010B/1461